MW01236209

Relief From Burnout

Manage Workplace Pressure, Set Non-negotiable Boundaries, and Restore Your Motivation

M.H. McKinley

The Page Press

Preface

"In dealing with those who are undergoing great suffering, if you feel 'burnout' setting in, if you feel demoralized and exhausted, it is best, for the sake of everyone, to withdraw and restore yourself. The point is to have a long-term perspective."
~ Dalai Lama

We live in an environment which has developed an unhealthy tendency to romanticize "hustle culture". Fetishizing constant, tireless work at the expense of our health and personal lives has robbed us of our personhood. Despite giving it our all, we unrealistically demand more of ourselves than our place of work. We have grown accustomed to treating ourselves as robotic cogs in a machine seemingly designed to slowly wither away our well-being.

In today's fast and furious world, everyone's lives are run by the engine of desires. Everyone has their desires, goals, destinations. Some want to be successful; some want to be rich; some want to buy their dream car; some want to own a huge house. The list of wants is limitless. To acquire these wants, people start running like a horse, too fast to reach their goals too soon. Somewhere in the middle of their race, they forget to rest, thereby over-pressurizing themselves.

Just like there are limits to everything, our body has its limit too. When our body crosses its threshold, it starts giving warning bells. It warns us to take rest, to take good care of ourselves, to keep our body healthy, and so on and so forth. If we refuse to take the signs seriously, we ultimately lose control over not just our body, but our mind as well.

When we are too focused on wanting something, we exert pressure on ourselves to achieve it, but what we fail to see is the negative impact our pressure has on our body, physically, mentally and emotionally. One such negative impact is burnout.

Burnout in technical terms, is a condition resulting from 'chronic workplace stress'. It is when our body is extremely exhausted and has reached its threshold. Whether you are a working individual, a housewife, a student, regardless of what we are or what we do, at some point of time in our life, we all experience burnout. But not many are aware of what burnout is, let alone know how to identify it and overcome it.

Though burnout affects everyone, it is more commonly and highly seen in working individuals, both employee and employers. In employees, burnout is seen when you experience extreme stress, feel exhausted, demotivated to work, lack of enthusiasm, whereas in employers, it affects their company's productivity and performance, causing them stress, fatigue, and other serious health issues.

In 2011, António Horta Osório, the CEO of Lloyds Banking group collapsed due to extreme exhaustion at work. He then decided to take a two-month break before he returned back to handle his company.

Just like him, there are many people who have taken time out of their busy life to prioritize their health before work. Had they prioritized their work and side-lined their health issues, it most probably would have affected the productivity of their business.

Both productivity and time management are negatively affected by burnout. When you are mentally exhausted, emotionally drained, and physically unable to focus on your work, it lowers your performance and thus affects the productivity of the company.

When you lack zest towards your work, you are most likely to procrastinate, lose track of your plans, and fail to accomplish your goals. Thus, causing a setback to your time management.

In today's world, depression is no foreign word. The word is known and experienced by almost every grown-up. Depression is when we feel extreme levels of sadness, and lack of hope in life. There are many reasons as to why one experiences it in their daily life. Many understand its seriousness, but not many acknowledge it in themselves and are ready to both face it and solve it. There are various symptoms of depression such as insomnia, fatigue, mood swings and etc.

Burnout and depression are undoubtedly related to stress. Though they both have similar symptoms, they are not the same. And you'd be surprised to know that extreme burnout could lead you to depression.

Though burnout affects us immensely, it can be overcome by identifying its symptoms, acknowledging them, and readily facing them through a few simple and easy methods. Relief From Burnout - Manage Workplace Pressure, Set Non-Negotiable Boundaries, and Restore Your Motivation presents a lucid blueprint to nurse your stressed, overworked self back to a happier version of yourself.

Contents

Introduction

On a frantic Friday evening, Laura walked briskly away from her desk to grab another cup of coffee from the employee's lounge. She'd barely had four hours of sleep last night, as usual. Coffee was her BFF. As she poured herself another cup, she happened to glance at the clock on the microwave. It read eight forty-two. She heaved a long sigh. Avery, her six-year-old daughter, would have finished her dance recital twelve minutes ago. Avery had begged her to be there for her first performance, but it had fallen on the same weekend as her project's deadline.

Even though she knew that she couldn't possibly have left work to be there for Avery, Laura still felt a pang of remorse. She ambled back to her office, and as she flopped back on her office chair, she noticed the screen on her phone was lit. There was a new message. It was a text from her babysitter, Kristen. "On the way to Baskin-Robbins to celebrate. Will be home around 10 pm," read the text. Attached to the text was a flurry of photos from Avery's first performance.

Laura didn't know whether to be happy, angry or even jealous, to take it a stretch. Happy that her daughter at least was having fun, unlike her sad self. Angry that, as a mother, she couldn't be there to witness her daughter's special day, and jealous that a babysitter was enjoying the beautiful moments and making memories with her daughter. It should've been Laura with her daughter, not some babysitter who was getting paid to be there. The worst part was that she had no one but herself to blame for her own miseries.

Laura put her phone aside and stared blankly at her monitor. She was far from being done and was way beyond exhausted. There was no way she would be able to get out of there by ten, or even midnight, for that matter. This was going to be another late-nighter at the office. Laura fisted her palms in frustration, shutting her eyes tight, and took a deep breath before opening her eyes again.

Though Laura had wanted to be at Avery's dance recital that night more than anything, it just wasn't possible. Instead, she had promised to be there at her next recital. But by this point, they both knew her words held very little weight. She had said the same thing when Avery had her piano recital a few weeks ago, when she participated in the school play two months ago, and even for her granny and grandad's 50th Anniversary surprise party that Laura herself planned.

But in the end, work always took the driver's seat of her own life. She became a mere passenger, bargaining for a better ride. Laura knew she needed to break out of this vicious cycle. But how? She needed the money; there were bills to pay. "*Why bother looking for another job?*" she thought. The next job would likely be the same. She just could not see a way out of her situation. It was like she could see the door that would get her out, but didn't have the keys she could use to actually unlock it and walk out.

Do you find yourself relating to Laura's situation? Are you living a similar life? If so, you are not alone. In fact, you are actually a part of the majority. You'd be surprised to know that, according to APA's 'Work and Well-being' survey conducted in 2021, around 79 percent of employees experienced work stress. Due to this, they faced negative impacts in their work field, such as lack of interest, motivation, energy [26 percent], and lack of effort at work. [19 percent]

These findings aren't exactly new. This is infamously known as burnout! But what exactly is burnout? Are there any symptoms? More importantly, how do you save yourself from burnout and find relief from its effects? The answers to these and many more can be found within the pages of the book that you are holding, 'Relief From Burnout: Manage Workplace Pressure, Set Non-negotiable Boundaries, and Restore Your Motivation.'

What can you expect from this book? To begin with, we will learn to differentiate between stress, depression, and burnout, regardless of their similarities. Then, we'll expose one of the catalysts to burnout: workplace cultures and practices that incentivize burnout. Next, we will explore possible triggers of your burnout through a self-examination. In the later chapters, we'll help empower our mindset towards a positive change.

With renewed strength, we'll be able to "Draw the line in the sand," as we call it, and set some overdue boundaries. Finally, in the last chapter, we will fortify with self-care tools to help restore and maintain balance in our life that we can implement right away. By the end of this book, we hope to be able to conquer burnout, equate success in life with personal fulfillment, and find deep satisfaction in our improved lifestyle.

Let's get started.

Chapter 1

Demystifying Burnout

"The greatest enemy of knowledge is not ignorance; it is the illusion of knowledge."
~ Daniel J. Boorstin

Have you ever seen a duck on a pond? How gracefully they glide through the water, propelling themselves smoothly like it's what their bodies were made to do. Who would've thought that beneath such adeptness and efficacy lies the constant struggle of incessant paddling to stay afloat. We're all like ducks, constantly struggling to make ends meet, with a constant sinking fear of drowning. We might look to be in control and productive, but inside, we are becoming more of a mess with each passing day.

Laura's life was much like that duck on the pond. Her daughter, Avery, would sit by the door, eagerly awaiting for her mother to return from work. Every day she waited, just so she could tell her mother all about her day, the fun she had, and how well she did at school.

But the moment Laura would walk in through the front door, Avery would take one look at her mother's tired and exhausted face and it would diminish all of her excitement. Laura would barely make it to her bedroom at times. There were days when she would just plop her bag on the couch and fall asleep right there. As much as Avery wanted to jolt her mother awake and fulfill her desires, she didn't have the heart to disturb the sleep that her mother needed so desperately.

With hopeful eyes, she'd then wait for her mom at the dinner table, but by then, she would either be fast asleep or busy on her phone talking about business. Relentlessly, Kristen, her babysitter, would serve her dinner, and by the time Laura returned, Avery would be off to bed or busy with her schoolwork. Avery would watch her mom scroll through her phone while hurriedly finishing her food, and in the blink of an eye, she would be back to working

It wasn't just Avery that faced the short end of the stick. Avery often overheard her dad arguing with her mom on how she has changed, she has no time for them, and how he has had enough of her missing out on their life citing work pressure. Once, her mother came home late for her own parents' anniversary celebration. Avery's dad was so mad at her that, he didn't talk to Laura for a month straight.

Avery agreed with her father's complaints. Laura missed out on so much of their lives. With each passing day, she began to see less of her mom. Avery believed that she and her dad had disappeared from her mom's busy life. Amidst all of this, weren't Avery and her dad missing the big picture? Wasn't Laura doing all this for them? Wasn't she working hard, day and night, just so she could provide a better life for them?

Laura was slipping away from their lives because she wanted to see them get ahead in life. But what good was that when she wasn't even there to enjoy the present with them. That's when Avery and her dad decided to take things into their own hands. They decided to talk to her and have her understand that while her work was important and they appreciated how hard she worked for them, but her presence in their lives was much more important.

Though Avery was too young to know what 'burnout' was, she knew that her mother's presence was worth more than anything else she could possibly bring to the table. Laura, on the other hand, was so busy meeting one deadline after another that she didn't realize what was happening to her. Yet, deep inside, she knew she was missing out on her daughter's life.

Like Laura, oftentimes, we all go through phases in life not knowing what it is. By the time we realize what is happening to us, we are too caught-up the webs of life. Unless we are able to identify what our problem is, we won't be able to find a solution. And without solving this problem that's affecting our life so greatly, we are left feeling stuck as we aimlessly struggle through it.

The problem that we most commonly face in our day-to-day life is, 'burnout'. But before we delve into solving it, let's take things one step at a time. Let's first understand what burnout is, the cause of it, and how we can gain control over it.

What is Burnout?

Just like the tranquil duck swimming swiftly in a pond, a person suffering from burnout may look like they have everything under their control. But actually, they are tirelessly laboring to keep themselves afloat. This endless toil of strenuous labor without adequate breaks eventually leads to burnout.

In technical terms, burnout is an emotional state born out of exhaustion that often leads to physical and mental health issues. It is seen extremely commonly in workplaces. Contrary to what most people believe, it does not affect just millennials. It's an epidemic that affects people of all ages and professions. It is not exclusive to a particular gender or age group; it affects anyone and everyone who faces a particular set of straining situations, like work, parenting, or relationships.

In 2019, the World Health Organization (WHO) defined burnout as an "occupational phenomenon" and "not a medical condition," with the hopes that it would address the misconception of burnout being insignificant and assist in validating people's suffering and symptoms.

According to neuroscientistNeuroscientist Dr. Judson Brewer, Director of Research and Innovation at Brown University's Mindfulness Centre, said that burnout can mean many things to many people. He believes burnout is basically exhaustion and detachment.

In simpler terms, burnout is a feeling you experience when you feel mentally overwhelmed, emotionally drained, and physically unable to fulfill daily needs. It doesn't necessarily have to be work that leaves you burnt out. You can experience it in a variety of fields in life.

We experience stress for an extended period of time at home, at college, and in relationships. What we should be aware of, is that such extended stress could lead to physical ailments and bodily diseases, such as anxiety and depression.

Common Symptoms of Burnout

Laura experienced various symptoms of burnout. Some of these symptoms were blatantly visible to the eyes while others were not. The visible symptoms are seen in various forms, such as physical, emotional, and behavioral changes in the individual. Let's consider a quick overview of some of the more common symptoms attributed to burnout.

Physical Symptoms of Burnout

Some of the many symptoms that we experience during burnout is frequent headaches, easily falling sick, sleep deprivation, and body aches. We may sideline them, chalking it up to feeling under the weather or something we ate that didn't agree with us. What we don't realize is that we are experiencing the physical symptoms of burnout. These are just some of the many symptoms, but there are plenty of others such as:

- Feeling drained or lethargic most of the time

- Frequent muscle pain or headaches

- Change in sleep habits or diet; loss of appetite

- Reduced immunity

- Forgetfulness

- Loss of concentration

- Diseases and illnesses

These symptoms are so common that one could easily mistake them as being symptoms of some other illness or even consider it as part of their daily routine. These symptoms may sound simple, but their adverse effects can be lasting if left uncared for too long. Fortunately, the solutions to these symptoms aren't all that hard to practice.

When we feel tired or lethargic, it could be our body giving us a sign that we need to improve our health. It doesn't always require us to follow a strict diet program. It may be as simple as needing to drink more water more often. It could also include incorporating healthier choices in our diet, like reducing our caffeine intake or incorporating healthy amounts of sleep into our schedule along with adding several relaxation activities into our schedule.

One such change could be taking a walk post dinner for a few minutes. Walking, especially after dinner, aids in both digestion and relaxation. Meditating for a few minutes every morning could also give a good kick-start to the beginning of our day.

Emotional Symptoms of Burnout

Do you often experience terrible mood swings? Do you sometimes feel irritable, pessimistic, or resent having to go to work? These are clear emotional symptoms of burnout. More such symptoms are mentioned below:

- Self-doubt and a sense of failure

- Feeling depressed, defeated, and helpless

- Lack of motivation

- Feeling detached from the world

- Apathy and dissatisfaction with work

- Feeling lonely

- Reduced sense of accomplishment and satisfaction

- Increased negativity and cynicism toward work

- Losing empathy

- Feeling stuck

When we pressure ourselves to accomplish too many tasks within a short period of time, we vent dissatisfaction with not achieving these goals in the form of self-doubt and cynicism, which often leads to feeling depressed, lonely, and loss of motivation.

There are circumstances where, despite being knowledgeable and skillful, we believe that completing a task that is within our capabilities is not our cup of tea. A little voice in our head hinders us from moving forward. Having these voices that feed negative thoughts to us isn't wrong but *giving in* to these voices and accepting defeat without giving something our best shot is wrong.

Instead, when faced with self-doubts, we should think about how far we have come. If we have made it this far, then we can definitely cross the hurdle that is presently blocking our way. We can practice positive thinking to overcome self-doubts.

Behavioral Symptoms of Burnout

Sometimes, we are prone to blowing up and shouting at others for silly things. There would be times when we would holler at our loved ones and immediately regret our behavior. Despite acknowledging it as wrong, we refuse to talk to others about our problems, which are also some of the behavioral symptoms of burnout. Some of these behavioral signs include:

- Relying on drugs, food, or alcohol to cope

- Inclination to distance yourself from others

- Taking your frustration out on others

- Procrastinating

- Being late for work and wanting to leave early

Instead of distancing ourselves from people and deciding to brave all our problems alone, we should talk to those who are willing to listen to us. Sharing our problems may not always solve them, but it definitely helps us to feel lighter. And sometimes, it can even help you find the solution you need.

When shared with others, the solution to a problem can be discovered because of the differing perspectives that others can offer. Remember Iam Tongi, the winner of the 2023 American Idol? Initially, he wanted to quit singing because he would hear his late father singing alongside him during certain songs. Feelings of grief would overwhelm him, making it difficult for him to get through a song. His mother consoled him by providing him with a fresh perspective. She asked him to try and view his father's voice as positive reinforcement. With this new and positive perspective, Iam was able to overcome the hurdle that stood in his path and continue his journey toward reaching his dream goal.

It's wrongly believed that our issues can be reduced or will disappear if we rely on using drugs, alcohol, or food. Sure, getting addicted to such things for brief periods of time may help us forget our problems or why these problems exist for a little while. But what happens after we come back to reality? The problem is still there - unresolved and growing in magnitude.

Instead of relying on such "quick fixes" that serve us no good, or ignoring them, we should courageously face them. The sooner we are able to sort them out, the quicker we will be able to get rid of them.

Consequences / Symptoms of Occupational Burnout

At times, constant exhaustion, lack of sleep, and irritability are the consequences of occupational burnout. Job burnout can be manifested in various ways. Sometimes, before you can spot its triggers, you may already be facing significant consequences. The following are common consequences of job burnout, even in its late stages.

- **Overwhelming anger/sadness**: The most common symptom identified among people who battle job burnout at their job is uncontrollable sadness, anger, or irritability anytime they think of their job. They unknowingly, either bury their anger deep within, or vent them on those who had no hand in bringing out that side of them. During times like these, instead of speaking what comes to mind, we can take a deep breath, or count numbers from backwards to calm our emotions down.

- **Fatigue:** You may begin to find it hard to complete the simplest task around the office. Fatigue inevitably sets in when all of your time and energy is spent working, without taking any breaks or going on a vacation. This physical pullback will slowly block your mental state. As important as finishing a task within the deadline is, it is equally important to take breaks, and give our body and mind some rest.

- **Insomnia:** The human body needs 7-9 hours of uninterrupted sleep daily. Working overtime or with a variable sleep schedule can lead to decreased productivity throughout the day. Insomnia is the main cause of fatigue in humans. The more we force our bodies into working late hours by sacrificing sleep, the more harm we are causing ourselves, which leads our bodies to degenerate. Instead, we can practice meditation or breathing exercises to relax our mind, and thus relax our body in the process.

- **Susceptibility to illness**: People who work tediously, without a break, can easily fall ill, no matter how fit and healthy they appear.

Rather than working continuously for hours, taking a break every once in a while is highly encouraged.

Burnout vs. Depression

So far, we have learned what burnouts are, how we can identify them, and some simple tips on how we can overcome them. But do you know that there is something else that is very similar to burnout? Yes, it's called depression.

Depression is when we feel overwhelming sadness and lack interest in pursuing our daily activities. Does this sound like a symptom of burnout? Yes, indeed. Both burnout and depression can have similar symptoms. The physical indicators of burnout are almost the same as that of depression, but these medical illnesses are *not* the same. To complicate matters further, it is possible to experience both burnout and depression simultaneously. While there are many similarities between depression and burnout, there is a critical difference between the two. Even though burnout may lead to depression, depression does not cause burnout.

In the case of burnout, you can take a day off or two and feel somewhat refreshed. Whereas with depression, taking time off won't make a difference. The overwhelming feelings of sadness and hopelessness will still be present. Seek medical help if you or your loved ones feel that your condition may be clinical depression.

(Note: To complicate matters further, it is possible to experience both burnout and depression simultaneously.)

Transitory Stress vs. Chronic Burnout

Stress! Have you felt nervous while giving a presentation or when you were asked to speak in public? Or how about when taking an important exam? We experience stress in different aspects of our life. Despite having the knowledge of what to say and how to deliver, we are overcome by stage fright and wonder *what if* we make a fool of ourselves in public. Despite our intense studying and knowing the syllabus well, we worry about *what if* we end up forgetting the correct answers, thereby failing the exam. These *what-ifs* block our paths even before we start off.

Stress is a way our body reacts to extreme pressures, whereas burnout is a condition that results from extended distress.

People often mistake stress and burnout to be the same. Furthermore, scientists have affirmed that they are related, especially when one involves the symptoms. However, stress and depression are different medical conditions. Stress is an integral part of life that you cannot do without. However, stress should not increase to the point where you feel as if your world is turned upside down. When it gets to that stage, the severe stress has likely resulted in burnout. As a result, it becomes harder to control one's anger, sadness, guilt, and other negative emotions. Extreme stress may often lead to burnout.

The Burnout Contagion

Having a poor working environment and work-life balance can lead to burnout. But did you know that burnout is also contagious? Burnout can sometimes spread slowly from one dissatisfied employee to the next. Other times, it can spread like wildfire, especially when there are unfavorable changes to the company.

When your co-worker, leader, client, or boss is experiencing burnout, there's a high chance that you subconsciously fall prey to it too. It happens as a result of interacting with them frequently. We interact with our peers for various reasons, such as seeking help or sharing doubts. These interactions influence us strongly, both emotionally and mentally.

Individual Transmission

Physically speaking, when we are close to a sick person who has a fever, cold, or any other contagious disease, we are prone to getting infected as well. Similarly, burnout can spread too. An employee's negative attitude and unproductive work ethic can set a negative example for others to follow suit. On the other hand, it can also indirectly impact their colleagues as they are left to pick up the burned-out employee's slack, thereby increasing their own workload. This chain reaction over a prolonged period eventually causes them to experience burnout themselves.

Group Transmission

Burnout can also be transmitted within departments or even throughout the company. A survey conducted by researchers, Michael Leiter and Christina Maslach, says that "emotional exhaustion" is a major aspect leading to burnout. When a company conducts mass layoffs, restructures, brings in new management, or implements policy changes, it often negatively impacts the mental health of its employee. Negative emotions such as fear, confusion, or frustration develop among employees. These emotions spread like wildfire from one employee to the next, thus starting a vicious chain reaction. If these feelings are not addressed and dealt with appropriately by workplace management, it leads to complaints and gossip among the employees.

Restructuring

Restructuring is when a company decides that they need a new structure for financial or legal reasons to uplift the company's profits. When companies restructure, there will always be some positions that are no longer useful or needed. The employees who occupy such positions risk losing their job in such situations, and many end up unemployed. This may have adverse effects on the remaining employees, as their workload is oftentimes increased. When the restructuring process is mismanaged or lacks communication, employees may start to feel that their hard work does not yield any awards or benefits, which leads to feelings of demotivation and dissatisfaction in the workplace. The company's decision may instill a sense of unfairness and injustice among its employees.

Change of Management Team

After having worked in a company for an extended period of time, employees develop a sense of comfort and understanding among their peers and higher-ups. When a new set of people emerge as the leaders in an organization, there may be an entire overhauling of the company structure and working terms which entails new rules, work ethics, and standards. Having a new leadership style and policy can be difficult for many, especially when the previous leadership has been successful and is what everyone is accustomed to.

The change of management may just be for the well-being of the company, but it sets the employees back in terms of comfort in the workplace and elicits feelings of confusion and ambiguity. Employees may experience a lack of control over their tasks due to new leadership and management.

A Gradual Process

Laura's condition didn't get worse overnight. It was a slow and gradual change that began with small things like not enjoying work anymore, not wanting to go to the office anymore, constant exhaustion, and many other such symptoms. Seemingly insignificant symptoms like these soon pile up and form a mountain of setbacks that feels almost impossible to climb. This is what causes people to get burned out.

Burnout is a gradual process. It can slowly erode your well-being, until one day, everything overwhelms you. Pay attention to these red flags and take action immediately before you have to face a full-fledged burnout. Here are some questions to ask yourself to determine if you could be experiencing a possible burnout.

- **You feel disconnected from your job and have lost interest in it.**

Have you lost your joy or the positive vibe you used to feel at work? Do you lack the motivation to go to work? Do you resent being at work during your time there?

- **Your productivity and performance are declining.**

Is your performance less stellar than when you started your job? Are you just doing the bare minimum required for your job? Is your work no longer a choice but the only option?

- **You constantly feel exhausted.**

Do you feel drained and left with little energy to do anything when you get home? Even on the weekends, do you feel like staying cooped up in your room?

- **When every day is a bad day.**

Does it feel like something seems to go wrong every single day without fail?

- **When you feel like nothing you do matters, makes a difference, or is appreciated.**

Do you feel unheard and unappreciated? Do you feel like your efforts go unnoticed or are unimportant?

- **You have difficulties falling asleep.**

Do you suffer from insomnia or sleepless nights? Are your thoughts or worries keeping you up at night?

- **Caring about your home or work life seems like a total waste of energy.**

Are you starting to care less or feel less motivated to keep your home tidy? Do you believe that going to work is a waste of time?

- **Days feel overwhelming or mind-numbing dull.**

Do you notice things that occupy most of your time are not inspiring, motivating, or worthwhile?

- **You struggle to distinguish between one day and the next.**

Do you feel like your days are blended together, making it hard to distinguish one day from another?

- **You rely on booze or drugs to get through the day since it is difficult for you to focus.**

Do you turn to booze or drugs as a coping mechanism to forget your misery? Have your family members or friends been expressing their concern for you?

If you can relate to some or most of the symptoms mentioned throughout this chapter, the first thing you must know is that you are not alone and that you can get yourself out of this rut with help. You have already taken the first and maybe the most challenging step, which is not ignoring your situation. Keep moving forward and do not give up. If you encounter setbacks, which is completely normal, give yourself some grace and do not be too hard on yourself. Burnout is not entirely all on you, as we will find out in the next chapter.

Chapter 2

Fanning the Flames of Burnout

"The willing horse is always overworked."
~ Charles Darwin

T ANYA HAD ALWAYS BEEN a hard worker. Her work was her primary source of pride and joy. She was always willing to go the extra mile to get things done. But lately, her boss had been pushing her to work even harder. He assigned her more tasks than any other employee on her team.

In the initial phases, Tanya was excited. She saw it as an opportunity to prove herself and advance in her career. She worked long hours, skipped lunch breaks, and took work home with her at night. She barely had time to see her friends and family, but she didn't mind. She was determined to succeed.

But as time went on, Tanya started to feel the pressure. She was constantly exhausted, both physically and mentally. She was constantly stressed out and anxious and had trouble sleeping at night. She started to feel like she was sacrificing too much for her job. She questioned whether her sacrifices are worth all the stress they cause.

Despite her exhaustion, her boss continued to push her to work harder. He would call or email her late into the night, expecting her to respond immediately. He would give her impossible deadlines and demand that she meets them.

Tanya tried to keep up, but it was getting harder and harder. She found herself making mistakes and struggling to concentrate. Her colleagues noticed that something was wrong and questioned her regarding the same, but she didn't want to admit it. She didn't want to let anyone down, especially her boss.

One day, Tanya hit a breaking point. She was working on a project for days, barely sleeping or eating, and it just didn't seem like it was going to come together anytime soon. She felt like she was drowning, and she couldn't take it anymore.

One day, Tanya's boss called her into his office. He told her that she needed to work even harder and that she wasn't meeting his expectations. Tanya was devastated. She had given everything to her job, but it seemed like it was never enough. She tried to explain that she was doing the best she could, but her boss was unsympathetic.

Tanya left the meeting feeling defeated. After having dedicated herself entirely to this job, she deserved more than a little leeway and sympathy from her boss. As she walked out of her boss' office, she realized that he was indifferent towards her health and needs. She had been pushing herself to the limit, sacrificing her well-being for a job that didn't care about her.

That night, Tanya had a breakdown. She cried for hours, the feeling of failure stinging her hard. She couldn't understand how her boss could be so cruel and insensitive.

The Toxic and Glorified Culture of Hard Work

If you have ever experienced work pressures similar to Tanya's, then you are probably very familiar with the toxic culture of hard work. While harmful in itself, its *glorification* is even more destructive. Most companies are not satisfied with just par workers; they want workers that are wholly dedicated to the company in mind, body, and soul. Sadly, the performance of individuals or workers who work within the contract is perceived to be the bare minimum and ordinary.

"The harder you work, the more successful you'll be. You must make many painful sacrifices to get to the top." Have these words ever been said to you? Despite the popularity of these words, does anyone know where we have to draw the line between being efficient and overzealous?

I once saw a tweet from a popular ride-sharing company that made a shout-out to one of its drivers, who was nine months pregnant. While having contractions, the driver took one more transportation request before heading to the hospital. She was revered for her dedication and 'hard work'. I wonder what the company wanted to achieve with that advert. Did they want other workers to make similar sacrifices? Would you? Was the driver's decision even right for her health and condition?

We can readily recognize the promotion of toxic hard work through the many slogans we often hear, such as:

- Your hard work will pay off

- Work harder than ever

- There's no shortcut

- Work hard, no matter what

- Hard work is the key to success

- Hard work gives you a better life

- Success comes from hard work

- Don't take rest; just be the best

- Work more, get more

How is hard work by these standards seen as dedication rather than a health risk? Why do workers have to give up their lives for their company? What truly defines hard work? Does following this definition of hard work guarantee success? Is idolizing your work at the cost of putting your own health in jeopardy really worth it?

Remember what Mark mentioned at the outset? At the time, they let go of some of Mark's colleagues because they did not *exceed* their monthly targets consecutively. To meet such unreasonable demands, one would need to work long hours and neglect their health and family. In today's world, if you are not doing more, you are not doing enough. Have you ever wondered, "How much is too much?" Working into the late hours while sacrificing sleep, food, and peace of mind is too much. Prioritizing others' needs before yours is too much. Sacrificing your present to have a shot at a better future is too much.

This definition of hard work that has been inculcated in us is sorely outdated. Working more hours does not make you more valuable in the eyes of the company. Conversely, it depreciates your value. Instead, efficiency and consistency will get you to the proper attainment of success. You do not have to be miserable to be successful.Sometimes, it's not hard work but smart work that needs to be done.

In a recent study conducted by WHO (World Health Organization), and the ILO (International Labor Organization), it was found that long work hours increase the risk of death from ischemic heart disease (17%), and stroke (35%). To put it in simpler terms, people who work for extremely long hours are most likely to attain untimely death than by any contagious disease.

Common Work Ethics or Beliefs for Celebrating the Culture of Toxic Hard Work

Fifty-two percent of all workers in America work more than forty hours a week. We are conditioned to work from dusk to dawn. You'd be surprised to know that, according to WHO, 745,000 people died in the year 2016 from stroke and heart disease after having worked long hours. The answer to productivity is not hard work but finding ways to be efficiently creative. You cannot be creative about your work if you are in a constant state of exhaustion. Feeling burned out does not equate to diligence and efficiency. Nor is it the way to climb up the corporate ladder.

In fact, I have witnessed people being replaced by their colleagues who didn't work anywhere close to as hard as they did. Understandably, they felt cheated and mistreated because they honestly believed that their hard work and overtime would eventually pay off.

We are constantly bombarded with work ethics that ultimately work against us instead of for us. Let's go over some of these shared beliefs.

It Is the Way to Success

We have been taught that working hard will help us to advance in our career. But does this principle actually apply in real life? Apparently, not. We sink deeper into the abyss of stress and depression when we subject ourselves to extreme pressure.

Some believe that in order to get noticed, you must work overtime. However, a staggering number of people work hard for years and still find themselves in the same job position that they were in years ago. But working hard does not promote development and growth, which are essential to success.

The notion that "Hard work is the way to success"has often led people into succumbing to depression, anxiety, and loss of peace. It even has adverse effects on relationships. In their urge to reach a destination called success, people tend to forget the notion that actually holds true, "Success is not a destination, but a journey."

We will see in a later chapter what it truly means to be successful.

It Denotes Dedication and Expertise

We often find ourselves sacrificing our work breaks and social life to focus on our work as we believe that it would help us to achieve a greater level of success in our career. But, in the end, do our efforts yield the results we desire?

Many people confuse hard work with dedication, as they believe it goes hand in hand with dedication. However, this is nothing but a misconception. Dedication means being committed to your goal, whereas hard work is the effort you put into completing your tasks. You can absolutely be committed without being overworked. A committed person is focused on a course of action, such as achieving growth and positive results, but they do not need to overwork themselves to accomplish this. Remember, balance is the key to all things.

It Pleases the Boss

One of the main reasons for us to work hard is to impress our boss. We feel that proving to them our skills and work ethics will increase our chances of securing a promotion or even an increase in payment. But, in the end, is being in their good books worth putting your mental health at risk?

Overworking yourself may please some bosses, but it is a short-lived experience, lasting only till the day you are considered valuable. A company I used to work for would emphasize that everyone is replaceable. If you do not bring anything innovative to increase revenue for the company, someone else will. Let's not forget that we are a replaceable asset to our work. We are only good and of any value to them until we satisfy their needs.

It Will Lead to a Pay Raise

Yes, money does wonders. Yes, money is a necessity. More often, we wish to advance in our career mostly because it would result in an increase in our pay. It is a common belief that working more leads to better chances of being promoted.

I have seen countless people work in the same position for years without a pay raise, or at best, a minimal one. Most hard-working employees are not offered a significant pay raise at their current position unless they move up the corporate ladder into a new position. Companies are constantly looking for ways to cut costs because increasing profits is their main goal. Thus, increasing a staff member's pay rate would work against their primary objective.

Red Flags to Note

Starting a new job can be exciting and energizing. A new workplace, new sets of people, lots of experience, and too many memories to make. It represents endless opportunities. However, very often, these feelings die within the first few weeks or months of working there. The 40-hour work week mentioned upon hire soon turns into a 50-hour work week, and sometimes even more. Requests for time off are repeatedly denied. You begin to notice a change in your behavior. Your health begins to deteriorate, you start to question your abilities and skills, you display a visible lack of enthusiasm and zest toward your job. The high turnover rate at the company is now glaringly noticeable. All of this, however, is not unavoidable. There are ways to spot symptoms of a stressful and toxic work environment before it gets to you. So, here are some red flags to take note of before you end up in the clutches of transparency.

Absence of Transparency

Many of us welcome transparency in a relationship. But what is transparency? Well, transparency, in definite terms, is openness, communication, and accountability. At the workplace, it implies that the person leading your place of employment should be clear about what your work entails, its expectations, and the goals they expect you to achieve. Lack of transparency is one of the most glaring signs of a toxic workplace. Sad as it is, according to a survey by the Edelman Trust Barometer, 58% of employees worldwide are skeptical of their employer. There is a common misbelief that withholding truth equates to "protection" for the person from whom the truth is withheld. Transparency is vital to building trust, and trust is essential to elicit feelings of security in the workplace.

Without transparency, employees start to believe that their work is undervalued, causing uncertainty and distrust to arise in their minds. An efficient way to tackle this block is through communication. Communication is the key to every relationship, it is also the key to resolving strained relationships between an employee and an employer when there seems to be an absence of transparency.

When the employer starts sharing information about your role, responsibilities, and gives valuable feedback, it develops a sense of confidence and trust among employees. It also motivates employees to work with greater enthusiasm.

Little or No Recognition for Your Work

Recognition — A singular, simple word, yet it holds a lot of weight. As an individual, regardless of what your skill and talent may be, if it's not recognized and appreciated, you'll either be stuck under the bridge of self-doubt or retreat back into the hole of uncertainty.

When workers don't receive recognition for their efforts, it diminishes their enthusiasm and morale. Little or no recognition contributes to job dissatisfaction and is also one of the leading causes of employee resignations. Why would anyone want to stay in a place where their efforts are either being condemned or not being recognized at all?

No matter how good the pay for a job is, it's been shown that workers who seldom receive recognition for their work will eventually leave. Employers and good managers should always take note of their team members' contributions, no matter how big or small, and reward them accordingly. Quarterly or annual reviews are excellent periods to recognize an employee's work in addition to discussing any problems that they may be having.

Being recognized in a workplace helps employees to realize that their work and contribution to the company is being valued. It also boosts the growth of trust, confidence, and respect in their employer.

When They Expect You to Always Be Available 24/7

I once saw a post on social media where a staff member took a snapshot of a note posted on the door of her workplace. The post read something along the lines of, "Overtime is to be expected, requests for time off will be denied for the time being, and on their scheduled day off, they are required to be accessible via phone. Additionally, the call *must* be answered, otherwise, disciplinary actions will be taken when they return to work." Needless to say, that post drove many commenters into a frenzy.

Being expected to be available 24/7 at work affects the employee's mental health and hinders personal relationships. When you are constantly on the lookout for when there could be a call from work that requires your attention, you hesitate to make time for yourself or for anyone else. You eventually begin to lose out on important events in life. Additionally, having to work all day every day could lead you to be burdened with excessive workload.

If you have ever been put into that position, you know how extremely frustrating it can be. You feel like you can never really unwind due to fear of being called in to work at any given moment. Even though they are your employer, it is unreasonable for them to expect you to be tethered to your desk or phone all the time and work at their whim.

Excess Workload

Having a workload that matches your mental strength and physical ability ensures productivity and satisfaction. But when you are overloaded with work that is beyond your capabilities, speed rather than quality often takes precedence. Your thoughts will constantly be on the work that is yet to be done, and tasks that have already been done will oftentimes be overlooked. Excessive workload could make you feel overwhelmed, which in turn makes you unable to focus on the task at hand. You become exhausted both physically and mentally. This stress puts you in a fight or flight mode and clears the way for burnout to take over your life.

According to a survey conducted in 2017, 60 percent of workers were concerned about work pressure that seemed to gradually increase in the past few years. They were concerned about the excessive workload and impending deadlines.

Constant Fear of Failure in the Workplace

No one likes to make mistakes, whether at work or in any other walks of life, yet they are exceedingly common. Some of the most important learning experiences come from making errors. If you are shown disapproval or annoyance for your honest mistakes, especially minor ones, let that be a sign of caution. Working for a company that does not allow room for any mistakes is definitely a red flag. Even worse is working for a company that diligently reprimands those who have made a mistake. Perfection is impractical and impossible to expect from any human being.

As Winston Churchill once said, "*Success is not final, Failure is not fatal: it is the courage to continue that counts.*" The fear of failure has a firm grip on our minds, holding us back from moving forward in our life. When you feel afraid of failing, ask yourself these questions:

- What are you afraid of failing at?

- Why are you afraid of failing?

- What is the worst that could happen if you fail?

- What is the best that could happen if you succeed?

Your answers to these questions may help you guide your way out of fear and lead you to firmness and positivity.

Why Toxic Positivity Is Harmful?

Another toxic culture in the workplace is toxic positivity. Toxic positivity is when someone tries to suppress, avoid, or invalidate another person's thoughts or feelings of despair rather than offer empathy. Toxic positivity doesn't always have to come from someone else; more often than not, it could come from our own self.

In a survey that was conducted by Science of People, it was found that 68 percent of people experienced toxic positivity just merely a week into their job. What was even more surprising was that 75 percent of people had never even heard of the phrase "toxic positivity". Not many people are aware of what toxic positivity is in the first place, so knowing how it affects their mental health is a long shot.

Recall any painful moments in your life when you opened up to a close friend, family member, or workmate. What was their response? Did they try to one-up your story by telling you their or someone else's experience that was worse than yours? Or maybe they replied, "What doesn't kill you only makes you stronger." No doubt, they all meant well. But these experiences are examples of how positivity can turn toxic.

Instead of undermining someone's problem and telling them, "Don't worry, it's common", acknowledge their issue and offer realistic support. If you are unsure about what to say to make them feel better, it's alright, but don't say something that could belittle their suffering or make them feel like their problems don't matter.

A Cheerleader That Won't Stop Cheering

It's easy to recognize and dismiss toxic positivity when we hear it from another person. But when those same words come from our inner critic, it could be incredibly challenging to recognize or dismiss them. It could push you further into the black hole that you are trying to escape from.

Having the strength and courage to deal with our thoughts and feelings openly is essential. Surely, this is easier said than done. A key component is to deal with it in a positive and productive manner. Rather than letting the negative thoughts get to our head, replace those negatives with positives. Instead of sitting down and saying, "It is impossible, I can't do it", try saying, "It is possible, I can do it."

Later on, in the final chapter of this book, we will address how to cope with difficult emotions through self-compassion. For now, we will discuss some signs to try and determine if we may be using toxic positivity on ourselves unknowingly, and what we can do to overcome it.

Poker Face

Poker face is usually a term used to describe someone who shows no emotions on their face. When we see someone who reflects no signs of emotions, we come to the conclusion that they are either too strong or emotionless. But is that really the case? Not at all. It's just that people with a poker face are very good at pretending that everything is fine and feigning indifference.

Have you ever pretended that everything is good, even when it is not? You might have felt that you didn't want to burden others with your problems, or maybe you were raised in an environment where emotions such as sadness or anger were discouraged. Repressing or avoiding difficult emotions is like leaving a wound unattended and hoping that it will heal all on its own.

Instead of suppressing our emotions and feelings, seek the help of a loved one, be it a family member, a best friend, or anyone whom you believe will not judge you. Talking out loud about what's bothering us may not solve the problem, but it can definitely reduce the severity of the problem at hand.

Overly Optimistic

Do you tend to make light of your problems by brushing them aside or making a joke of it, yet inside, you are hurting?

A few years ago, a friend of ours lost his mother. We expressed our condolences, and to our surprise, he was nonchalant about it. He even proceeded to make a small joke. We were amazed at how well he was taking things. That was until we spoke to his wife, who gave us a completely different story of how he was coping behind closed doors.

The widely known phrase, "Don't judge a book by its cover," holds true surprisingly often. Oftentimes, an overly happy face is not a happy soul. We believe that coping with our problems by not taking them seriously makes it easier to solve them. Instead, we are trying to ignore the reality by living in a make-believe world.

Optimism is good, but over-optimism can lead to overconfidence, ignorance, and poor decision-making.

What You Can Do to Overcome Toxic Positivity Personally

Understand That It Is Okay to Not Feel Okay

We all go through ups and downs in life, and it's okay to feel sad or anxious when you're down. You do not need to feel guilty, embarrassed, or ashamed for having those feelings. Acknowledging your feelings instead and allowing yourself to feel those emotions is a healthy way to heal and move forward.

Instead of believing that not being okay is wrong, start believing that "It is okay to not be okay".At the end of the day, we are all human beings. It's okay to have an occasional bad day, to make mistakes, and to want to let your emotions out. It's all part of being human, and it's definitely okay to be human. We absolutely are not alone in this. We have our family, our friends, and all of our well-wishers who will support us and stand with us.

Share Your Feelings and Concerns

It is okay to share your concerns and grievances with others when you're not well. It doesn't make you less of a human if you do, and trying to cope with it all on your own doesn't make you a warrior either. Having an extra pair of hands on the job always makes it easier to win the war.

If you feel like you can't talk to anyone or don't feel comfortable doing it, then talk to a piece of paper. Yes! Journal your thoughts, your feelings, and your daily activities. Writing may seem like a tedious task to some, while some may feel the same about talking to others. Choose however you wish to share your feelings, but never convince yourself that there's no one to talk to or that no one will listen to you. There's always someone.

FOMO: The Fear of Missing Out

The fear of missing out is widespread among people of all ages. The pressure to perform just as well, or to outperform others, is intense. Social media is a major contributor to FOMO. Well-meaning posts can give off the vibe that you are missing out on everything you could ever want (i.e., the dream vacation, a brand-new car, dinner at a fine-dining restaurant, etc).

I recall this particular year vividly when I saw a friend post a photo of her trip to Paris on social media. Not long after, I saw another couple post their trip to Italy. This continued with five or six other mutual friends posting about trips to Europe throughout the next year and a half. Have you noticed the same within your circle of friends? I can already see your head nodding.

At times like this, we often find ourselves looking for whoever is enjoying the same privileges. We start to question ourselves, "Why am I being left out?" "When will I ever be able to do things like they are?" Sometimes, in fear of FOMO, we force ourselves to do things that we are usually not comfortable with. We start watching series that do not match our interests simply because others in our group are watching it, and we fear that we'll have nothing to add to the conversation or feel like an outcast.

The fear of missing out can affect not only our personal life but also our work life. How did you feel sitting in that company meeting where colleagues were recognized and awarded month after month, with your employer passing you off as if your efforts meant nothing? FOMO un-doubtedly breeds competition and jealousy instead of teamwork and unity.

The fear of FOMO at work could affect our productivity and performance. Feelings of jealousy or the ill thoughts that we harbor in our mind to be better than all of our colleagues will end up affecting our working relationship with them.

So, let's discuss steps to avoid being influenced by such a toxic work culture.

How You Can Avoid Being Influenced by the Toxic Work Culture

Unfortunately, the competitive nature of today's world has made people forget about what a healthy work-life balance should look like. We could avoid the ill effects of burnout if we know a few workplace practices.

Set Boundaries

In order to please our boss and prove ourselves, we take on more and more work that goes far beyond our capability, and we sacrifice our personal life to complete that work. But what we fail to do is set boundaries with our work and our boss.

When it comes to work relations with your supervisors and subordinates, you need to know where the line is and recognize when it is being crossed. Harmless or not, you must have the courage to voice your opinion clearly and concisely without an aggressive tone or manner.

The subject of setting boundaries will be discussed more thoroughly in Chapter 5.

Quit Glamorizing Being a Workaholic

When we view our job as our pride and joy, we readily sacrifice everything, even when those sacrifices cost us an arm and a leg. We fail to notice that our willing nature to do anything for our job is one of the key reasons for our burnout.

It goes without saying that the culture of "working hard" is deeply ingrained in the American ideal. We are told things like "busy means successful". However, this culture is no longer acceptable when it compromises your productivity, family life, and health.

I once worked for a company where the CEO worked himself tirelessly till the day of his retirement. He missed out on family events and quality time with his children in exchange for working at the office. Once he retired, he found himself in a home filled with silence and emptiness. He tried to rebuild his relationship with his children and grandchildren, but it was challenging. They were still harboring feelings of resentment for his lack of presence since their childhood.

Be Well-Versed in Labor Laws and the Code of Conduct in Your Company

When we are employed by a company, we often neglect to read up on our state's labor laws or even our company's contract. This opens up the possibility of our higher-ups or our boss exploiting us.

For example, in America, according to the Fair Labor Standards Act of 1938, the minimum wage was set at 25 cents per hour, which in today's dollars price, is equivalent to $4.60. Similarly, every state has its own labor laws that are made to protect its workers from exploitation. It is essential to be knowledgeable about these laws that are meant to look after your well-being.

When you are well-versed in your state's labor laws, it will be easier to identify duties or conducts that go beyond or against your contract. Review your job responsibilities from when you were hired and determine if their current requests are within or outside those guidelines. When you are ready with your case, address your concerns with someone from upper management.

An important thing to note here is that you will always find colleagues who do more work than they're required out of choice. Do not feel pressured because of it, you are not bound to do what they do.

Quit Trying to Please Everyone (But Yourself)

Despite having already crossed the exhaustion line, we sometimes push ourselves to continue working simply because we are afraid to disappoint our boss as well as our colleagues. So, we agree to take on extra work. But do you feel like in the pursuit of pleasing others, we're losing track of our own well-being?

Do you find yourself saying yes to almost everything asked of you and feeling guilty about having to say no? When you say no, do you feel the need to provide an excuse or reason even when they haven't asked for it? While there are good sides to wanting to please others, there's also a major downside if balance is not exercised.

We all have limited time and energy. Figure out what your priorities are and stick to them.

Do Not Compare Yourself to Others

The desperate urge to advance in our career often leads us to take on more work than others are willing to. We believe that by working more than others, there is a greater chance that we could get promoted faster than our colleagues.

When you compare yourself to others, you are using another person's standards to judge yourself by. Instead of comparing yourself to others, why not focus on your personal goals and development? Concentrating on your personal development will bring you inner satisfaction and true joy. By making the necessary improvements, you will ultimately increase your value. More importantly, you will avoid the spirit of competition and find true inner contentment.

As Theodore Roosevelt said, "*Comparison is the thief of joy.*" By comparing ourselves to others, we are indirectly handing them the reigns of our happiness. Instead, in moments like these, we should replace the negative thoughts that harbor in our minds with positive ones.

Normalize Saying No

Tanya, mentioned at the outset, refused to reject more work due to her wish of not disappointing others. But in the end, she ended up disappointed in herself.

If the required task will eat into your personal time or health, be empowered to say no or negotiate new terms that would be favorable to both sides without compromising your values.

Saying no occasionally doesn't automatically make you a maverick. On the flip side of the coin, feel free to say yes to tasks you are willing to do beyond your comfort zone but are still within your personal limits. In doing so, when the time does come for you to say no, your rejection will be taken more seriously, and it will be easier for them to respect your newfound set of boundaries.

Don't shy away from saying no, because, as novelist Anne Lamott said, "'NO' is a complete sentence." It's okay to say no, even if it displeases others. It is better than saying yes and placing yourself in a distressing situation.

Do Not Skip Breaks

In order to accomplish our goals faster, we often skip necessary breaks at work. We believe that in the few minutes of break, we can catch up on our work. But this actually leads to more exhaustion for us, both physically and mentally.

You are not alone if you have ever felt guilty about taking a break from your work. Some people fear being judged by their coworkers even for taking a break, especially if said coworkers do not take breaks themselves. It's crucial to push past these emotions and self-comparisons and take breaks when you need them.

Recognize the benefits of taking breaks, such as better and more efficient work performance. Try adding reminders on your computer or mobile phone to alert you when it's time to take a break.

What About You?

Now that you know what an unhealthy workplace looks like, it's time to think about yourself and your workplace. Read the following questions and ponder over them for a while.

- How many hours were you supposed to work for according to your contract? And how many hours are you actually working for?

- Does your boss often force work upon you? And do you often find it hard to refuse the work?

- Have you ever been appreciated or praised for your work?

- How does your boss react if you end up making a genuine mistake?

- Does your office tell you to be available 24/7? Do you often get calls and emails outside of work hours and are told to respond to them ASAP?

- Do you often skip your breaks in hopes of completing more work?

- Is it common for you to compare your work to your colleagues' work? Do you fear what will happen if you are not able to work as much as, if not more, than others?

Once you find genuine answers to these questions, you'll recognize when something needs to change or whether or not your workplace ethics are amiss. Granted, we all can't move to Mars to get away from the influence of a toxic work culture. But what we can control is deactivating anything that can set us off and raise our stress levels. Let's find out what those triggers are as we do some soul-searching in the following chapter.

Chapter 3

Getting to the Heart of the Matter

"When solving problems, dig at the roots instead of just hacking at the leaves."
~ Anthony J. D'Angelo

E MMA HAD BEEN EXPERIENCING profound exhaustion and a lack of motivation, to the extent that she was finding it difficult to complete even the most basic tasks. She was teetering on the edge of burnout, fully aware of her deteriorating state.

Initially, Emma attributed her struggles to an overwhelming workload. She had been taking on more and more responsibilities, trying to prove herself to her boss and colleagues. However, despite her efforts to scale back and prioritize what truly mattered, the sense of burnout persisted, refusing to dissipate.

Upon reflection, Emma gained a new perspective and realized that the company she once held in high regard was engaging in actions that clashed with her own moral compass. In an effort to disguise the company's mistakes, Emma was instructed to lie to the client and deny any accountability. This did not sit well with her. She also noticed that the company seemed to prioritize profits over people and that greed was a motivating factor in almost all business decisions.

Emma felt torn between her affection for her job as well as the relationships she had formed with her colleagues and the nagging realization that her workplace contradicted her personal values. This internal conflict further intensified her uneasiness.

If you've ever been in a predicament similar to Emma's, you can understand how distressing it is when your personal values are constantly being challenged. Sometimes, it might be difficult to pinpoint the underlying cause of your burnout because we don't readily consider our incompatible values as a cause. Additionally, there are usually several factors that could be attributed to our burnout. Now, let's delve into some of these potential factors.

Work-Related Triggers

Unsurprisingly, the workplace is the number one recorded place for burnout. Records show that 79% of new employees in a working office are likely to quit their jobs three months after being hired. The workplace is primarily about productivity. Maintaining high productivity usually requires workers to put in excessive time and energy with little rest. Companies that care more about profits than their people exhibit attributes in the workplace that have a negative impact on their workers.

While many workers were laid off during the pandemic, the others who had their jobs were assigned more work, adding to the already overbearing workload and pressure. If they refused, they could've lost their jobs, and if they agreed, it could cause them more stress than they already had.

Similarly, in Emma's case, the main cause of her burnout was her workplace. The excessive workload, coupled with their clashing ethics, is what caused her burnout. There can be many other workplace-related issues that can cause burnout. Let's see if you may be adversely affected by some of these common attributes.

Lack of Control

One of the main reasons for our burnout is our lack of control over our work. Just like Emma, we, too, are sometimes forced to lie when it benefits our company. On the one hand, we believe that it is our duty as the company's employee to work for its benefit. On the other hand, it goes against our personal work ethics.

Most instances of burnout in employees are caused by their lack of control over how a job is carried out. Do you have little or no say over your work? Do you feel like you are being micromanaged?

Lack of control can also be experienced if you lack the tools or resources to do your job. Are they outdated, not working properly, or not even provided? If you are faced with these same questions, it is better to get your doubts clarified by your employer.

Lack of Recognition

Vincent Van Gogh was a famous Dutch painter who revolutionized the history of art. Though his paintings are now extremely valuable and quite expensive today, his talent was not recognized during his lifetime. In fact, his work received so much criticism and ignorance that it led him to depression and ultimately to him ending his own life. Sadly, it was not until after his death that his work earned a name for itself.

Life is all about the incentives we get from doing what we do. So, when you are not given any credit or shown appreciation for your efforts, it can cause you to feel undervalued. And feeling undervalued can leave you unmotivated and unproductive.

Do your efforts go unrecognized or taken for granted? Did someone else receive all the recognition for the work you did or were a part of? Do you lack the desire to improve your skills or to seek advancement? Do you feel as if your supervisor keeps adding more tasks to your already lengthy list? Do they downplay the extra work as something superficial or something that could be done in very little time? Ask yourself these questions and if your answers are mainly yes, then it's probably a good indication that your workplace may not be a good fit for you at this time.

Lack of Fairness

When our employer acknowledges and appreciates the work of our colleagues but not us, it gives rise to feelings of self-doubt. When we take on extra work and complete it on time and still receive no appreciation or praise from our employer, it feels like our hard work and time were all for nothing. This treatment feels unfair, and biased, and is demotivating. It makes us feel like our boss has some personal vendetta against us.

Unfair treatment in the workplace can lead to decreased employee productivity, increased absenteeism, and, ultimately, a high turnover rate. Moreover, it often creates an environment of distrust and fosters resentment among both team members and upper management. Feelings of resentment can drain our energy and stimulate further negative feelings of anger and irritability.

Does it ever seem like a workmate is shown more attention and privileges than others, perhaps because of their ethnicity, gender, race, nationality, social status, age, or physical characteristics?

Lack of Support

When Emma was told to lie to her client, she expressed her hesitation to her boss. Instead of soothing her worries or taking her view of the situation into account, her boss just told her to not take it personally and simply to do as she was told. She felt like her words were unimportant and that her boss didn't consider them for even a moment.

When we face a similar situation, we may feel afraid of speaking against our employer to others as there's a chance that we could lose our job or, even worse, get black-marked.

Leadership that fails to take a sincere interest in their workers and their needs often experiences a decrease in morale and performance. In a poll by Webrecruit, one-third of workers attributed the lack of support from management as the most significant contributing factor to their lack of motivation to work. Does your employer have an open-door policy? If there is one, do you feel hesitant or apprehensive about discussing your concerns because you doubt that you'll be understood?

No Passion for Job

Eighty percent of the world's population says that they are in a profession they are not interested in. So, if your heart isn't into your work, you are not alone. But wouldn't you rather be in the 20%?

Research conducted by Career Vision showed that just 20 percent of working employees seem to be passionate about their work, whereas 33 percent reached a dead end in their work, and another 21 percent wished to change their career.

If you are still passionate about the line of work you are in but not about the company you work for, it might be time to switch over to a new company instead. If you are no longer passionate about your career as a whole, consider branching out into new adventures.

Out of Sync With Values or Long-term Goals

Every individual has a certain set of values and goals. But the desire to achieve their goals without forfeiting their values is not always an easy path to walk on. Just like Emma, there could be times when you are asked to choose between your values or goals.

If you choose your goals, you will have to sacrifice your values. One day, when you achieve your goals, more than the satisfaction of achievement, you will be filled with the guilt of having sacrificed your values for these goals. When you choose your values, your goals may seem distant but not unattainable. When you finally reach the destination through this path of values, the satisfaction of achieving your goal added with the joy of never losing sight of your values will make the journey worth it.

Working in an environment that aligns with your values is crucial to job satisfaction and happiness. Having a job that does not fit well with your long-term goals and personal values will make it challenging to be productive and feel committed to the job. Make a list of your values, with one column for the values you desire and another for those you dislike. Now, check off any values from both columns that would hold true for your current job.

Worries About Job Security

We often place ourselves in a situation that we regret later on simply because we are afraid of losing our job if we don't comply with our employer's demand. In Emma's case, the moment Emma was asked to lie, she felt compelled to comply despite having her own reservations. If she refused, even for something as valuable as her ethics, she knew that she'd be laid off sooner or later. Her values were paramount to her, but that didn't change the fact that she really needed this job. It wasn't until the guilt of going against her personal values hit her hard that she was forced to reconsider the situation.

Seventy-seven percent of people agree that worries about job security contribute to their burnout. Every worker is afraid of losing their job. If you're an entrepreneur, the fear of losing the market and not making enough sales is real. Determine if your anxiety is well-founded by considering some of these signs: Are you given fewer assignments? Are there new management or talks about mergers? Is your relationship with your manager elusive and unfriendly? Are you receiving more criticism about your work/job performance? Is the company having financial problems?

Dysfunctional Office Dynamic

When we always give our all to our job and rarely make mistakes, we expect to be appreciated and valued, which in turn motivates us to work harder and do better than before. But if our boss never has a kind word to say about us despite our excellent work ethics and quality performance, we feel demotivated and begin experiencing a lack of enthusiasm.

Most times, job stress happens not because of the job itself but because of the people involved. You may be the target of an office bully, feel undercut by a coworker, or have your job micromanaged by your employer. If you keep your emotions bottled up inside of you instead of confiding in someone, your frustrations will likely be expressed in other ways, such as being sarcastic or taking it out on someone who had nothing to do with you being wronged. Do you dream of ways to retaliate? Or do you find yourself hoping that that person will one day be let go or quit?

Stress From Working at Home

When we take up more and more work for various reasons like wanting to satisfy our employer's demands, proving ourselves to our boss, or wanting to do better than our colleagues, the allocated office time won't be enough. In order to complete it, we decide to take our work home and are ready to sacrifice our personal time. Taking work home not only hinders us but also hinders our relationship with our family.

Almost half of the UK's workers felt that working from home contributed to their burnout. For some, the environment at home stifled work productivity due to interruptions from family members or pets. Additionally, having and seeing work inside their home made it difficult for some to separate work and home life. Those in a single household felt that working remotely offered no social interaction and increased their loneliness and feelings of isolation.

Lifestyle-Related Triggers

Lifestyle-related burnout refers to the triggers that affect how we function in society. Burnout sets in when you become enslaved to patterns or lifestyle habits that keep you moving in circles without getting you anywhere. They drain your energy without providing long-term gain.

Lifestyle-related triggers include daily habits that we practice, most of which will be discussed below.

Letting Distractions Rule Your Life

Bonny had enough time during her break to log into her social media accounts and scroll through posts for a while. But she didn't realize that what she believed to be "a while" was actually her entire break. In addition, she was spending a lot of time on social media while "relaxing" at home.

Today's world is fast-paced. The distracting nature of technology or the hectic lifestyle of being a part of the global system can easily interfere with one's priorities. Studies show that the mobile phone is the leading cause of distractions today. Your brain can't get where it needs to be in order to expand if beeps and notifications constantly dominate your attention.

It's no secret that the growing technology has benefited society in many ways, but the same technology comes with undeniable cons. On the positive side lies access to vast amounts of information, whereas on the negative side, access to such information can be used in detrimental ways as well. Whether technology is a boon or a bane depends entirely on how we use it.

In 2021, a survey conducted by PRC (Pew Research Center) showed that 90 percent of Americans claim that technology was essential to them, especially during the pandemic, whereas 40 percent of people claimed to feel lethargic after spending extended periods of time on video calls.

Consider putting a time limit on your technology usage. It will also aid in helping you become more productive with your time and duties.

Dehydration and Intermittent Fasting

Aside from mental exhaustion, burnout can happen if you fail to establish a balanced eating schedule and a good diet.

In most schools, kids are taught to drink a minimum of six to eight cups of water. We may have followed it back then, but how many of us still follow it today? Not many. When our body gets dehydrated, we start experiencing all kinds of illnesses, from fatigue and dizziness to lack of metabolism. Many people avoid drinking water simply because it causes frequent visits to the restroom. But did you know that loss of water in our body can not only cause physical health risks but mental health risks as well?

It is essential to drink enough water every day to keep both mentally and physically fit. Have you ever wondered how to find out if your body has enough water? Well, you can find out by checking the color of your urine. If the color of your urine is dark yellow, it is an indication that your body does not have adequate water intake. If the color of your urine is clear, your body has sufficient water.

Intermittent fasting is the latest in the line of fad diets designed to help you get fit. Intermittent fasting, in simpler terms, is when you cycle between eating and fasting. You fast for a certain period of time, which is then followed by a period of eating, and then fast again. There are several ways of intermittent fasting. If done properly, it is quite beneficial. Some people, though, may experience fatigue and mood swings.

Eating on the run or failing to rehydrate regularly can wreak havoc on your health. Eating at your desk while continuing to work instead of taking a real meal break is also detrimental to your health.

For some lines of work, mainly those dealing with customers, your lunch break may be dictated by a rotating lunch shift between coworkers. That can be especially difficult if the person ahead of you starts or ends his lunch break later than scheduled, which can cause a domino effect for everyone else. Consider suggesting or requesting backup assistance from upper management during busy periods to help keep everyone's meal break on time.

Loneliness

It's common for people to relocate for work. Many people move hundreds or thousands of miles away from their family and friends. Their new work life keeps them busy, leaving hardly any time to socialize in their new locality. With a small social circle or none at all, they begin to feel lonely or homesick.

In 2021, a survey conducted by Hadley and Mortensen found that people who feel lonely at work are most likely to feel burnout. When you feel extremely exhausted and overwhelmed, it could lead to feelings of loneliness.

Aside from relocating, you don't necessarily need to be working in isolation to feel lonely. I used to work at a company with 1,000 employees, but it was full of cliques. Being a newbie, I was lost in the crowd. Therefore, loneliness isn't necessarily the absence of people; it's the absence of any social connections. Try interacting with at least one person at work for a minimum of 40 seconds every day. If you mainly interact via videoconferencing, try logging in 5-10 minutes before the meeting starts to converse with anyone who arrives early.

Poor Physical Health

Physical health is interrelated with mental health. When you are physically unable to complete a task, it indirectly affects your mental well-being. It reduces your ability to cope with stress, affects your sleep, and causes you to experience mood swings. Poor physical health is common among those who have a sedentary office job. If you have a job that requires you to sit for a prolonged period, make an extra effort to move around regularly. This also applies to those who exercise before or after work.

Try leaving your water flask in the lunchroom instead of at your desk to remind yourself to get up and increase your physical activity. If you're not in a hurry, try taking a longer route to return to your workstation or office. Even changing the way you sit at regular intervals can yield benefits.

Lack of or Sporadic Sleep Patterns

As mentioned previously, Bonny would spend long hours on her mobile scrolling through her social media accounts late at night. As a result, she barely got enough sleep, maybe 3 to 5 hours a night. Her poor sleeping habits were the reason why she ended up falling ill so often.

In order to function well, we need at least seven to nine hours of sleep. If the human body is deprived of the amount of sleep it requires, it adversely affects the functioning of both body and mind. Lack of sleep reduces memory power, weakens our immune system, and can cause a great deal of irritability and mood swings in people.

Sleep deprivation is such a common issue that the Center for Disease Control and Prevention has called it a public health epidemic. Anxiety levels increased by 30% in those who were sleep deprived for just one night, states a study from the University of California at Berkeley. Besides having enough sleep of 7-9 hours per night, continuous and deep sleep is equally important. Good sleep habits are essential to achieve this. Some of these habits include:

1. Going to bed and waking up at the same time.

2. Eliminating electronics two hours before bedtime.

3. Avoiding caffeine and alcohol 4-6 hours before going to bed.

Personal Relationship Issues

Joe had been married for six years and has a beautiful four-year-old daughter. He loved his wife and daughter more than anything. Lately, Joe was repeatedly getting assigned an extensive amount of work that didn't seem to come to an end. By the time he would get done with work for the day, he barely had any energy left to talk to his wife or play with his daughter. He felt unmotivated to go to work every morning or even to meet up with friends on the weekends. He simply didn't know what to do anymore.

Relationship burnout occurs when feelings of depression, exhaustion, or pessimism about their partner arise. Are you both constantly arguing and blaming one another? Do you avoid communicating? Are you un-motivated to make future plans together, like taking a trip or buying a house? Have you stopped enjoying your time spent together? Do you feel like giving up on your significant other or ending the relationship? If so, consider speaking with a relationship counselor or, at the very least, with an unbiased friend you trust.

Caregiving

Joe knew that he wasn't well. He knew that his work pressure had ex-hausted him both physically and mentally, but he just wouldn't talk to anyone else about it. The thought of sharing his feelings with his wife or friends did occur to him, but he didn't want to burden them.

Burnout often ensues when caregivers regularly do not receive the help they need or don't take sufficient rest. When caregivers get overwhelmed and reach their threshold of sustainability, it becomes difficult for them to focus on their daily tasks, they start losing interest in what they love to do, and sometimes they may even take out their frustration on others.

Do you feel overwhelmed by your responsibilities? Are you easily irritated or argumentative with the person you are caring for? Do you feel anxious about the future?

Asking for help without feeling guilty or ashamed is critical to preventing and eliminating caregiver burnout. Let others know you need help. You don't have to do everything by yourself. Make a list of your tasks and delegate any that are too difficult for you or that others are willing or able to do. You may want to research if there is any available assistance from your state or local agencies.

Parenting

Even though parents love their children, there are days when they feel exhausted by their role. Being a parent means being available for their kids 24/7, even when they themselves are exhausted. It is a round-the-clock task that requires a lot of time, inexhaustible energy, a tremendous level of patience, and so much more.

If you are a parent, then ask yourself these questions: Are you burned out trying to raise your child/children? Are you unable to obtain sufficient sleep? Do you find yourself guilty or helpless for not being available for your kids all the time? Have you ever felt the need to question your capabilities as a parent?

Raising children is no small feat, no matter how many there are in the family. If you feel burned out, rest assured that it doesn't make you a bad parent, just a normal one. Parenting brings many profound rewards and indescribable joys, but that doesn't change the fact that it's extremely challenging. Remember, it is okay to feel burned out. However, not doing anything about it when you get to this point is not a wise decision. Try to seek help, be it from your partner, friends, or even professional help. Seeking help does not make you weak. On the contrary, it makes you strong.

Aside from trying to balance work with home and school/sports activities and everything else that can make your head spin, there are different personalities, abilities, and needs that have to be dealt with daily. The stress increases exponentially if you are a single parent without additional support. Seeking external help to care for your children occasionally, even for half a day or a few hours, can yield rich rewards for your well-being.

Homeschooling Children

Homeschooling can be a wonderful experience for both child and parent, but it can also be highly stressful at the same time. The demands of homeschooling a child can be overwhelming and challenging. This is in addition to balancing daily responsibilities at home and other obligations. In fact, research shows that 67 percent of people identify homeschooling as a contributing factor to their burnout. If you've reached a similar situation, ask yourself the following questions.

Have you considered changing up your homeschool schedule? Have you considered adding more fun events into the schedule, such as field trips, walking, running, biking at a park, or even participating in dance classes? Changing your classroom environment can also be beneficial. Try studying on your patio, backyard, or at a park occasionally for a change.

Certain Personality Traits Can Contribute to Burnout

Every individual has a unique set of thoughts, feelings, and behavior, which in a nutshell is referred to as their personality traits. It plays a major role in shaping our character. Our personality defines who we are and what we do, and why we do what we do. These personality traits are just a manifestation of our personality in various forms. However, certain personality traits can actually contribute to burnout. People with these traits are more susceptible to burnout than others. If you notice any of your own habits listed below, don't worry, you're not alone. There are a lot of people who face the same issues as you.

Perfectionist

A person who has an overwhelming desire to be the best in everything they do is often labeled as a perfectionist. It is not wrong to want to be a perfectionist, but when your desire to be perfect crosses its limit, it has the power to consume us whole. Striving for excellence is commendable, but striving for flawlessness is not.

Do you view anything less than perfect as a failure? Are you bothered by minor details that are out of place but insignificant? Are you always trying to fix that "one more thing"? Do you feel like you may be judged if your work is not flawless? Do you readily spot imperfections and mistakes? Do you focus more on the end goal than the process? If any of these questions are hitting close to home for you, try implementing some strategies to reduce their negative impact. You could start by engaging in positive self-talk, ensuring that you don't compare yourself to others, and you create an environment where you feel accepted.

As Albert Einstein once said, "A *person who never made a mistake never tried anything new.*" So, remember that it's okay to want to be perfect, but it's okay to make mistakes too. These mistakes are an important part of life. They teach us how to be better at doing what we do.

Pessimist

I'm sure you must've heard the phrase, "The glass is either half empty or half full" at least once. If yes, then you must know what an optimist would say and what a pessimist would say. If you don't, then let me tell you. According to that phrase, if you were to place a half-filled glass of water in front of an optimist, they would say, "It's half full," meaning that they focus on the positive aspect of things. A pessimist, on the other hand, would say, "It's half empty," meaning that they focus on the negative aspect of things. In other words, how you perceive your surroundings influences your personality to the point of defining it.

A pessimistic person lacks hope and expects the worst to occur in all situations. Do you find it hard to believe that things will go smoothly? Do you fear the worst outcome even when there is insufficient evidence for thinking so? If you struggle with pessimism, know that you can change your thought patterns to include a healthy dose of positivity and comfort.

Type "A" Personality

Generally, the term "type A personality" refers to a behavioral pattern associated with competitiveness and impatience. People with this personality type highly value their time. They dislike wasting time and tend to multitask often without a break. They tend to keep working until the job is completed, giving little to no attention to how much time they spend on it, which causes stress and imbalance in their work and health. They may also react with impatience or irritability to anyone or anything that slows them down. These tendencies often lead to stress and burnout.

However, it is possible to get out of such situations when you find yourself stuck in them. There are many ways to cope with stress and overcome burnout by exercising, practicing meditation, and maintaining a balanced diet.

Being Passionate in the Wrong Way

Have you ever received the advice that "If you do what you love, you will never work a day in your life?" When we love what we do, we feel motivated to do more of it until it becomes exhausting to the point of feeling burned out. Paradoxically, this intense devotion can even result in a loss of passion for the very thing that sparked our enthusiasm in the first place.

Interestingly, individuals who are primarily driven by extrinsic factors such as status or financial gain in their job tend to be more susceptible to burnout compared to those who find intrinsic motivation through pride and contentment in their work.

Why Am I Experiencing Burnout?

Given below are some 'Yes' or 'No' questions. Let's go through them one by one together!

- I feel unappreciated at work.

- My boss is not fair to me.

- I am not fine with making a few small mistakes.

- I don't want to talk to my family and friends these days.

- I keep worrying about my job.

- I don't feel valued at my job.

- I often end up focusing on the negatives in my life.

As discussed earlier on in this chapter, there are many possible causes of burnout. How you've answered these questions can help you to pinpoint why it is that you're experiencing burnout. It's not unusual to have several root causes of burnout. The key to actually dealing with these causes is to address them instead of ignoring them. To do this, we must change our mindset first, which is the topic of discussion for our next chapter.

Chapter 4

Mindset Makeover

"A restless mind makes a problem of a resting body."
~ Mokokoma Mokhonoana

MEGAN HAD ALWAYS BEEN her own toughest critic. Even as a child, she would often find herself dwelling on her mistakes and feeling like she wasn't good enough. As she grew up and matured, her negative self-talk intensified to the point that it started impacting her life significantly.

In the workplace, Megan's inner critic particularly took a toll. She would berate herself for the smallest mistakes, even if they had no real impact on her job performance. When faced with critical feedback from her boss or colleagues, it would trigger a spiral of self-doubt and insecurity, further exacerbating her struggles.

Megan's negative self-talk extended beyond the professional realm. Her inner critic permeated her personal life as well. She would relentlessly criticize herself for the slightest flaws or imperfections, constantly engaging in unhealthy comparisons with others.

Despite the toll that her pessimism was taking on her mental health and well-being, Megan felt powerless to change it. She had always assumed that her self-criticism was simply a part of who she was and that she would have to learn to live with it.

Most of our stress is rooted in our mind, and it can seem as if there is nothing we can do about it. But the truth is that you can change your mindset to impact your beliefs and actions positively. Like Megan, we, too, may sometimes engage in negative self-talk and have self-limiting beliefs that prevent us from living our best lives. In this chapter, you will learn how to arm yourself with a positive mindset instead, realize the true purpose and meaning of work, and learn how to shift your perspective and aim for a healthier work-life balance.

A Meaningful Life Matters

When you have a purpose in life, you're not just going through the motions. You're doing something that matters to you. When working towards something bigger than yourself, seeing the value in everything becomes much easier. When you feel like your job is a waste of time, it can be hard to motivate yourself to do anything productive.

You can avoid burnout by embracing authenticity, meaning, and purpose throughout your journey in life. When living a meaningful life is your goal, you develop resilience, which can help you succeed in many aspects of your life. By focusing on the bigger picture of what truly matters in your lives—the "why"— you will avoid burnout. When you're committed to leading a meaningful life, you become okay with accepting the good along with the bad. Your focus is no longer on the good and bad in daily life, it is on making your life meaningful in the long run. Your mission can fortify you, promoting strength, well-being, and prosperity, even when faced with adversity.

To prevent burnout, individuals who strive for a meaningful life leverage their values, abilities, and relationships. Your values will keep you centered, focused, and grounded even when a disturbance occurs. You can allow yourself to feel those emotions without feeling guilty or ashamed when you are aware of and tuned into your feelings, cravings, and limitations. You can control your emotions and impulsivity without feeling overwhelmed by focusing on the bigger picture and what is meaningful to you.

Success vs. Fulfillment

Imagine that a team of employees is given an extremely important project to complete. Their boss and management are strict about it, and the employees know that the project is highly critical for the success of the company. The employees do not spare day and night to work on the project and are quite successful with it. As soon as they are finished with the project, they immediately start to work on their next project. What is your opinion on these employees and their boss? Is their approach of working tirelessly actually effective?

Have you ever paused to ask yourself why you have been putting so much into your career or business?

We were sold on the prize for reaching excellence, and we believed in the notion that happiness comes from mastering our profession. We were instilled with the belief that only if we work tirelessly to accomplish some far-off objective will we be content. Despite these beliefs, countless individuals find themselves discontented even after achieving success in the workplace. It is now that they're realizing that success alone cannot define one's existence. This persistent sensation of dissatisfaction leads to pressure and worry. The pursuit of success and the fear of failure become deeply intertwined, inseparable like two sides of a coin.

Difference Between "Success" and "Fulfillment"

Is success and fulfillment the same?

The world often defines success as the attainment of fame, wealth, or social status. It is commonly perceived as a positive outcome, a triumph, or a victory. Our culture has placed a strong emphasis on achieving results, comparing ourselves to others, competing with them, or judging ourselves based on what we think will make us happy. The prevailing narrative encourages us to continually strive for more, acquire more, and become more. The focus is not just on becoming successful yourself, but rather on becoming more successful than others.

What is fulfillment? The Oxford English Dictionary defines fulfillment as the "Satisfaction or contentment as a result of the complete development of one's potential." The Cambridge Dictionary eloquently puts it as the "Feeling of pleasure and contentment because we are happy with our lives."

Though success and fulfillment are not the same, they can co-exist. There are people who are both successful and live a fulfilled life. At the same time, however, not all successful people live a fulfilled life, and vice-versa.

Ultimately, there is no universal key to success or some sort of shortcut to attain fulfillment.

Happiness is subjective to the person who acquires it. Each of us has unique interests, wants, and aspirations, and every person fulfills them in distinct ways. The key to finding fulfillment is to have a mindset that enables you to pursue the things that matter the most to you and achieve goals that align with your values. Therefore, to feel fulfilled, it is essential to consider what is meaningful to you and involve them in your life more fully. Honoring your true ambitions and desires will allow you to experience a sense of originality, purpose, and wholeness in your life.

Imagine a man who is doing what he loves, and while the job does not make him a lot of money, he does get to spend a lot of time with his family and friends. He is quite happy with his position, as he has almost next to no work pressure. Now, compare this man with the employees mentioned earlier, who'd been working under high pressure, with strict orders, and within a highly restrictive deadline.

How do they differ? Which one of them will you associate with "success"and "fulfillment"?

Which Should You Pursue: Success or Fulfillment?

The American culture considers achievements and accolades as a measure of success. We don't have to look very far to find someone who has succeeded in attaining the world's view of success. However, despite the glory associated with such achievements, they do not always lead to a sense of fulfillment for the individuals who attain them.

Many people believe that success is an all-or-nothing approach. Some assert that pursuing work that one loves will naturally bring about happiness, contentment, and a sense of significance. However, this notion does not always hold true in practice.

We rarely experience true peace, either professionally or personally, because our actions and goals are always judged by the success we can attain. This explains why being present is challenging when you're on a "podium". Additionally, once you've accomplished a goal, the carrot moves forward. Once a goal is accomplished, the focus swiftly shifts to the next objective, causing previous successes and pleasures to fade into the background. The problem with the hustle culture of today is that the hustle never stops, and many people, unfortunately, consider this to be a good thing.

When you see the work culture and the definition of success today, you might ask, is it even possible to find contentment in what we do? Absolutely! Numerous studies reveal that high-powered individuals who reported feeling true satisfaction did so by consciously imposing limitations. The cure for society's addiction to endless "more" is simply saying, "I have enough." Viewing it this way enables you to find satisfaction and contentment regardless of your choice.

Finding Genuine Success

In its true sense, success should not override fulfillment because they're supposed to go hand in hand. Therefore, it is vital to understand and identify genuine success. Only then will you be able to pursue fulfillment alongside success.

Genuine success honors your values, fulfills your personal needs, and rewards you with contentment. Do you remember what that study with those high-powered individuals revealed? It unveiled that those who consciously set limitations by acknowledging that they "had enough" were the ones who discovered true satisfaction. It takes inner strength and self-control to resist the constant chase for the "next carrot" and instead find contentment in the present moment. Embracing this mindset allows for a balanced approach to success and fulfillment.

What is considered "enough" will differ from one person to the next. You can now understand why we said that fulfillment is subjective and what it entails differs for everyone. It is essential that you define what success and fulfillment mean to you based on your objectives and standards, and not those of others. Materialize what success means to you by taking the time to sit down and write which goals support your personal values. Focus your efforts on things that provide you with happiness, a sense of success, service, and advancement. You can set both short-term and long-term goals for yourself.

Once you have a clear understanding of what success means to you, make it a daily commitment to work towards that success. Through consistent actions aligned with your vision, you will move closer and closer to your goal until the day you achieve fulfillment and happiness.

Changing the Way You Talk to Yourself

Megan was very harsh on herself. She criticized herself constantly, blamed herself for the smallest things, and had no issues speaking badly about herself. She was her own biggest enemy. Overtime, if we keep feeding negative thoughts into our mind, our thoughts manifest into reality. You will become an antagonist in your own story and will become the very reason why you're not happy or satisfied with what you do.

One of the secrets of achievement is the way you talk to yourself. How you see yourself can have a profound effect on your attitude, behavior, and how you view the world. Your inner voice and thoughts can significantly affect you. If you make it a habit to criticize yourself, call yourself names, and pass judgment on yourself, you'll soon start believing the things you say, even if they aren't actually true. Be aware of such tendencies and counter those thoughts with a positive mindset. Let's discuss some habits to establish a positive mindset.

Be Mindful of the Things You Tell Yourself

You might be surprised by how frequently you criticize yourself. Self-respect and confidence are essential to accomplishing your goals. If you claim that you're unqualified for the job or that your competitor will be offered the position, it will show through to others. Only by cultivating a positive image of ourselves in our own mind can we project this positive image to others and inspire confidence in our capabilities. By doing so, we can gain the trust of those around us.

So, be mindful of what you tell yourself. Feed positive thoughts to your mind and practice self-affirmations. Start your day with a fresh mind and positive thoughts.

Think It Over, Then Move On

Once you are aware of your inner voice, the next step is to rephrase those hurtful words into uplifting and constructive ones. So, think of positive words to replace these negative thoughts instead of leaving your mind and thoughts empty. Add these useful positive expressions to your vocabulary:

- Can - "I *can* handle it."

- But - "I don't know much about it, *but* I can learn it."

- Yet - "I cannot reach $10k....*yet*."

- Am - "I *am* intelligent. I *am* strong."

- Used to - "I *used to* be a tardy person, but I am getting better with my time."

- Next time - "I wasn't able to meet my quota this month, but I will do better *next time*."

Channel the Negative Into the Positive

Self-criticism can be beneficial if it motivates you to solve a problem, be in charge, and make things go as planned. However, more often than not, self-criticism causes you to doubt yourself, saps your motivation, and leaves you feeling helpless. It prevents you from being the best version of yourself. When your self-criticism is toxic, channel it towards being constructive.

Instead of saying, "I will never understand this," replace it with something more realistic like, "I don't understand this now, but I can try again later when I can focus better."

Additionally, try to focus on the action that produced the undesirable result versus the person who carried out the act. Instead of saying, "I didn't make the sale probably because I was being too pushy," say instead, "I didn't make the sale probably because I said XYX. Next time, I will say ABC instead, which sounds less intimidating." It is easier to change your course of action than to alter one's entire personality. Moreover, focusing on actions propels individuals toward their goals of success.

Human Giver Syndrome

While it is true that "There is more happiness in giving than in receiving," it does not encourage limitless giving. Just as one shouldn't donate their entire bank account to charity while neglecting essential financial obligations like mortgage or rent payments, it is important to find a balance in giving.

Similarly, giving more of yourself, by way of time and energy, than you can afford to give will not amount to making you happier. On the contrary, it will end up being detrimental to your health and well-being.

Some people give a lot of themselves to assist others, all at the expense of their own well-being because they feel that it is their moral obligation to do so. They have what is called the Human Giver Syndrome. Many people attribute the human giver syndrome to women, especially mothers, but many males are affected by it as well. It is essential to recognize that self-care and establishing healthy boundaries are crucial for both men and women to maintain their own well-being while still being able to help others.

Do you find it hard to say "no" to people? If someone has a need, do you push yourself to fulfill that need, no matter the toll it takes on you? Do you feel the need to make sure that every single person around you is happy? While compassion is an admirable trait to cultivate, it is crucial to recognize that exceeding our physical and mental capacities in demonstrating compassion can have negative consequences on our health and can contribute to burnout.

The Mentality of Needing to Keep Up With the Workload

I once mentioned my exhaustive to-do list to a friend and wondered how she, who had a heavier workload than mine, handled hers. She worked full-time in the medical field, and when she got home, she cared for her special needs child, who needed round-the-clock care. Her reply to my inquisition was, "Just do what you can." It was a simple answer, but it was a powerful statement.

Do what you can, and don't fret over what you aren't able to complete. Sometimes, we can be so hard on ourselves for not having everything crossed off our to-do list. Furthermore, in thinking about the things that we weren't able to do, we end up ignoring what we did achieve throughout the day as if it was undeserving of recognition.

Know When to Push Yourself, When to Slow Down

Granted, there are times when you need to push yourself a bit more, but if you are consistently in overdrive and rarely on cruise control, it's time to look under the hood. The notion, "if I push myself beyond my limits, I'm one step closer to success" will oftentimes backfire and push you ten steps behind instead. When you try to exert too much pressure on yourself, it adversely affects both body and mind.

Piling up too much on a plate that's too small, and then trying to consume it all will ultimately make you physically sick and mentally weak.

Here are some questions to ponder if you are doing too much. Do you find yourself rushing from A to B? Are you always multitasking? Do you constantly need help finding misplaced things? Are you falling behind on minimal chores at home (i.e., washing dishes, laundry, floors, etc.)? Do you get sick often? If so, it's probably time to ease off the gas pedal by eliminating or delegating some of the tasks on your list.

Brain Overload

Brain overload, as the name suggests, happens when too much information is dumped onto our brains. The brain ends up trying to process much more than it can handle. Since we are living in the 'Information Age', we are constantly being inundated with much more info than ever before from all directions. From the media to social posts, blogs, webinars, emails, etc, our brains are constantly trying to figure out what is fact and what is fiction. When our brains are overstimulated, we experience brain fatigue.

Jean Baudrillard, a French sociologist, said, "We *live in a world where there is more and more information and less and less meaning.*" When we overload our brain with too much information, it decreases the brain's ability to make proper decisions, or in other terms, causes 'decision fatigue'.

According to Daniel Levitin, a neuroscientist, "When our brain is fatigued, it becomes poor at making good decisions on important matters." It is critical to allow our brain time to rest and renew itself. A daily dose of mindful meditation, listening to music, power naps, nature walks, or simply taking a break from technology can all be wonderful ways to give your brain time to rejuvenate.

Negative Beliefs About Self-Compassion

When we are on the brink of burnout, we may not be aware of it actively, but we need to take a break We may even go so far as to consider taking a few days off from work to help us feel better, but later on decide against it since taking a break is inaccurately attributed to being lazy either by ourself or those around us.

Before we divulge into the negative beliefs surrounding self-compassion, let us first understand what it really is. Compassion is having sympathy or sadness over another's pain or suffering. When the feeling of compassion is directed at ourselves, it's called self-compassion.

There are a lot of negative beliefs about self-compassion. Some people think self-compassion is a weakness or a sign of weakness. Others believe that self-compassion is irrelevant or that it won't help them in their work or career. Is it true? Absolutely not.

The truth is that self-compassion is an essential tool for managing stress and dealing with burnout. Studies have shown that people who practice self-compassion are less likely to experience negative emotions and stress. They're also more resilient in the face of stressors (situations where we are extremely stressed).

Self-compassion helps us to focus on our strengths and weaknesses calmly and objectively. It allows us to see the situation from a more balanced perspective and make changes that will help us cope better with stress in the future. To improve your productivity, mental health, and resilience, embrace the practice of self-compassion. It might not be easy initially, but it'll be worth it!

Defining Self-Compassion

Christopher Germer said, "*Self-compassion is simply giving the same kindness to ourselves that we would give to others.*" This is a reassuring thought for those who feel apprehensive about exercising self-compassion.

Compassion combines all attributes that are recognized as unquestionably good—kindness, benevolence, understanding, tenderness, mercy, empathy, sympathy, and a drive to help others. Therefore, it is regarded as one of the more admirable human emotions. Having compassion gives us a sense of purpose that extends beyond ourselves but improves our own mental health in the process. In reality, there is no distinction between compassion for oneself and compassion for others.

Self-compassion is a powerful tool that can help you manage difficult emotions. It's a way of treating yourself with kindness and understanding, even when you're struggling. Self-compassion can help you feel calm and in control, which is essential when dealing with difficult emotions. It can also help you cope better with stress and pain. In short, self-compassion is a critical ingredient in a healthy emotional life.

There are many ways to develop self-compassion. You can practice it by thinking about your own experiences with emotions - good and bad. You need to treat yourself like a human being who is trying their best and not be averse to feelings of sympathy toward yourself. You can also practice it by doing something for yourself, even when you don't feel like it. Lastly, sharing experiences with others can foster a sense of connection and support.

By practicing self-compassion, you will not only feel better emotionally, but you'll also be able to help others do the same. Whether managing one's own emotions or assisting others in doing so, self-compassion plays a vital role in promoting emotional health and fostering empathy.

Self-Compassion Can Be Learned

Self-compassion is a powerful tool that can be learned. It's a way of viewing yourself as you would a loved one - with kindness and understanding. When we're compassionate towards ourselves, it helps us feel more connected to our emotions and prevents us from hurting unnecessarily. It also allows us to set boundaries and take action when necessary.

There are many techniques for developing self-compassion, but the most important thing is to start with something small. Start by acknowledging your feelings - even the negative ones - and then try to understand why you're feeling them.

Imagine your friend comes to you and tells you how they've been having a bad day, a hard time, or how they're facing certain problems in life. Now, would you tell them that many others are facing bigger problems than theirs and that they shouldn't make a mountain out of a molehill? Or would you treat them like a human being and be sympathetic towards them, listen to what they have to say, and tell them that it is going to be fine and that you will be there to help them every step of the way? Of course, you will do the latter. When you can treat your friend with so much compassion, why can you not treat yourself as a friend and be self-compassionate?

Next, try to take some action to help yourself feel better. Merely acknowledging your thoughts and feelings and accepting them is crossing half the sea. Now, instead of letting these thoughts and feelings get to you and control you, see what you can do to change them. Once you start taking steps towards change, you'll be crossing the remaining sea. This could involve doing something simple, like taking a deep breath or talking to someone about your feelings.

Finally, keep practicing self-compassion. It will become easier and easier over time, and it will help you to manage difficult emotions more effectively.

How Self-Compassion Helps You

When you practice self-compassion, you become kind and supportive of yourself. When you fail, you make sure that you're not harsh on yourself and use it as an opportunity to recognize areas where you may need to improve. The motivational force of self-compassion comes from love. Self-compassion will help you see the areas that warrant improvement and allow you to confess your shortcomings more readily. Being self-compassionate increases our mental well-being, and when we are mentally fit, we become physically strong as well.

It improves motivation as well. For instance, self-compassionate people are less depressed and nervous than self-critical people, which means that their mental condition is more conducive to taking responsibility. Additionally, they have more faith in their capacity for success.

Self-compassionate people are less emotionally affected by their past errors and are more likely to accept personal responsibility for themself. Failure and setbacks will remain a fact of life. No matter what you do and where you are, failure and setbacks will always lie in your path. However, when you learn to exercise self-compassion, you will be more inclined to pick yourself up and try again. Life itself never gets easier, you just get better at dealing with it.

Abraham Hicks' Method of Manifestation - 17 Seconds Rule

Abraham Hicks— It is the name of a non-physical entity that is channeled by Esther Hicks and Jerry Hicks, American inspirational speakers and authors who are famous for their teachings on the laws of attraction.

Abraham Hick's key to happiness is "Whenever you feel down, pull out a list of things that are happy and successful in your life and focus on just one or two of them. Keep focusing on those things and allow yourself to feel good about them. The feeling will help you to overcome the negativity." This practice is predicated on the idea that positive thoughts are a form of energy that attracts success in all spheres of life, including health, money, and relationships.

One of Abraham Hick's famous manifestations is the 17-second rule. According to the 17-second rule, focusing on a thought for 17 seconds activates its vibration, and focusing on it for 68 seconds makes it powerful enough to turn it into reality. Pretty mind-boggling, huh?

Seventeen seconds may seem like a short time, but here's the caveat: During those seventeen seconds, no other thoughts are allowed to enter your mind aside from your focal thought. As you can imagine, it isn't easy to maintain a pure singular thought when other thoughts keep popping into your head at random times throughout. But it can be done!

How to Use the Law of Attraction for Less Stress

Follow these simple steps to the 17-Second Manifestation Method:

1. Have a positive thought. It is important to be free of any negative thoughts that could hinder your manifestation.

2. Close your eyes and visualize experiencing that desire. The positive thought should be in the present tense and reflect your desires.

3. Focus on the thought for 17 seconds, then let go. Your focus should be completely directed towards that positive thought.

4. Repeat the cycle three more times for a total of 68 seconds. Set a timer for 51 seconds or 68 seconds.

Other things you might want to incorporate alongside the 17-Second Rule include journaling and mood boards. Journaling will help you see your thoughts on paper and readily recognize any thought patterns that need to be adjusted. Creating a mood board will help you focus on your goals and stay motivated.

Finding Balance Between Work and Life

Mark used to be relieved that his office rarely engaged in online meetings, especially after work hours. He was more than happy leaving his work behind in his office and maintaining a healthy personal life. All of this changed when the lockdown happened. Now that working from home had become the norm, he felt more overworked than he ever had. The online meetings never seemed to end. It took Mark only a few weeks to realize that he had barely talked to or spent any quality time with his friends and family.

Just like Mark, many are in a dilemma where they face an imbalance between work and home life. Work-life balance is both time and energy-consuming. Sometimes, you'd be so drained that you fail to even notice what is happening around you. It gets even more difficult to handle when priorities between personal and professional life begin to clash.

In a study by Aviva, 41% of people considered work-life balance more important than salary after the pandemic. Even after the pandemic, working at home has become the new normal for many. Some work remotely full-time or as a hybrid. It's common these days to have a Zoom conference in your living room, to work from your kitchen table, and to check your email late at night in bed. It is easy to become so engrossed in your work at home that you forget to clock out or go outside for some fresh air and sunshine. Whether you have a family or live alone, work-life balance is crucial for everyone's mental health and physical well-being.

What is Work-Life Balance?

Imagine you are in Mark's shoes, spending all your time and energy on work and having little to no time at all for family. If your spouse, parent, or child questioned you about it, you might lash out at them or state matter-of-factly that all of your hard work is for them so that they can live a lavish lifestyle. But is the lavish life that's going to come someday in the future worth missing out on in the present? This is where work-life balance comes into the picture.

Work-life balance is the practice of creating an equilibrium between work and personal life. It is crucial to achieve this balance to maintain a healthy lifestyle and prevent burnout, all the while staying productive. Work-life balance is prioritizing work and home life and gaining a sense of harmony between the two. This can mean different things to different people. Still, it generally involves making conscious decisions about spending your time and energy to maximize happiness and well-being.

To have a successful work-life balance, it is important to have a clear understanding of your priorities and values. This involves setting boundaries between your personal and professional life and effectively communicating them to your employer, colleagues, family, and friends. For example, you may decide not to answer emails after a specific time of day or to take a certain number of days off each month. Your employer must know about these decisions so they can also adjust their expectations accordingly.

It is also essential to establish a routine and stick to it. This can include setting a schedule for work, leisure activities, exercise, and rest. Setting aside time for yourself in your daily schedule is vital to achieving a healthy work-life balance. This can include reading, spending time with family, or participating in hobbies or exercise. Basically, you need to do something that makes you feel good and happy every single day without fail.

Maintaining a healthy work-life balance is not only beneficial for your physical and mental health but also helps reduce stress, anxiety, and burnout. It enhances your overall productivity, focus, and well-being. It can also help maintain relationships with family and friends and improve your overall quality of life.

Overall, work-life balance is an integral part of achieving success and well-being. By making deliberate choices and prioritizing between work and personal life, it becomes possible to strike a healthy balance. This can help to reduce stress, improve productivity, and maintain relationships with family and friends. Work-life balance is critical to achieving success and well-being.

Why is Work-Life Balance Important

A study showed that 83 percent of employees claim to have faced negative impacts in their personal life due to work burnout. Another study also showed that 72 percent of employees stated that a work-life balance is very important when looking for a new job.

Work-life balance is an important concept in today's society, affecting our personal and professional lives. We need to have a healthy balance between our work and home lives to be productive and successful. Work-life balance goes beyond just managing your time. This balance involves effectively managing energy, emotions, and stress levels, as well, so that your time can be used as efficiently as possible.

When we can effectively manage our workload and home responsibilities, we can lead a healthy and fulfilling life, enhancing our productivity and creativity in the professional sphere. By ensuring that our work and home lives are balanced, we can be more productive and less stressed at work. This can help us to be more successful in our careers and enable us to enjoy our lives more.

Achieving a work-life balance can also help us to stay healthy. When we manage to balance our work and home lives, we can also find time to exercise and eat healthily, which can positively impact our physical and mental health. Furthermore, by nurturing a healthy balance between work and home life, we can allocate quality time for our loved ones. This fosters strong relationships and emotional well-being, adding further value to our lives.

As you might have realized after considering Mark's situation, work-life balance among employees has worsened post-pandemic. The work conditions during the lockdown have not only increased the unhealthy competition in the workplace but it has also habituated people to work overtime at their homes.

There is a notion stating that when you practice something for 21 days, you will get habituated to it. Well, if that is considered to be true, then you can imagine how it would be for people who spent months-long working from home. The pandemic had a huge impact on everyone's lives, and its effects lasted post-pandemic as well.

In a survey conducted by Ipsos for the WEF (World Economic Forum), around one-third of workers were ready to quit their jobs if they were forced to work in-office full time. Despite its negative effects, the pandemic induced work-from-home culture did prove beyond any doubt that employers don't need to mandate coming to the office for their employees.

When we achieve a work-life balance, we can lead happier and more fulfilling lives. We can pursue our passions, whether we do it through hobbies, volunteer work, or other activities. This can help us to feel more fulfilled and content with our lives. Additionally, when we can maintain a healthy balance between work and home, we can better manage our stress levels and ensure we can live a healthy, productive, and successful life.

Overall, work-life balance is an essential concept in our lives today. By ensuring that our work and home lives are balanced, we can lead healthier, happier, and more successful lives. Work-life balance is not just about managing our time but also about managing our energy, emotions, and stress levels. It is essential to take the time to ensure that we can maintain a healthy balance between our work and home lives so that we can lead successful and fulfilling lives.

Work-Life Balance and Stress

Stress is a natural response to situations that can cause emotional or physical discomfort. Various factors, such as work deadlines, environmental factors, or personal relationships, can cause stress. Stress can harm your physical and mental health if not properly managed. It can lead to fatigue, anxiety, depression, and even physical illnesses over time.

In 2018, a survey conducted by Korn Ferry reported that two-thirds of its participants have sleep issues that are a direct result of work-related stress. In 2019, Dynamic Signal conducted a study called State of Employee Communication and Engagement in which it found that around 63 percent of employees claimed to quit their jobs due to work-related stress.

Creating a healthy work-life balance is essential for managing stress levels. Taking time out for oneself can help to reduce stress and promote mental and physical health. It is necessary to create a schedule that allows for both work and leisure activities to maintain a healthy work-life balance. This balance can help to reduce stress and improve overall well-being.

Positive and Negative Stress

Dan and Jay were two friends who studied at the same college. Though they were good friends, Dan was a top student, while Jay barely managed to pass his exams. They both applied for the same position at the same company and were selected for an interview. While waiting outside in the lobby, both were undeniably stressed. During their turns, both were asked the same questions, and their answers were also more or less the same. Jay maintained his confidence and barely remembered the interview questions. Dan, on the other hand, fumbled and stuttered throughout his turn. Who do you think would be selected for the position?

Let's look at the interview situation from the recruiters' point of view. Though Jay was academically lacking good scores, his confident attitude while facing the interview made up for his lack of grades. Dan, on the other hand, was a different story. Although he was a top student, it certainly didn't reflect in his interview. If you were a recruiter, who'd you rather choose?

Both Jay and Dan were equally stressed about the interview. The only difference here was that Dan was negatively stressed, whereas Jay was positively stressed. *Are there different types of stress? Yes!*

Stress is a normal and expected part of life, but its impact on our well-being and productivity can vary depending on the type of stress we are experiencing. Not all stress is bad. Positive stress, or eustress, is a beneficial form of stress that can motivate and energize. On the other hand, negative stress, or distress, can be overwhelming and debilitating.

Positive stress can be beneficial in motivating us to meet goals and deadlines and allowing us to experience new and exciting opportunities. It can also help us perform better as we meet the challenge. When you are positively stressed, you feel excited and motivated. For example, a student studying for an exam may feel the positive stress of wanting a good grade and work hard to achieve it.

In contrast, negative stress is a response to a situation perceived as threatening or overwhelming. This type of stress can be damaging to our mental and physical health and can lead to feelings of anxiety and depression. When you are negatively stressed, you are overridden with anxiety and lose self-confidence. Negative stress can be caused by an overload of responsibilities and expectations, a lack of support from family or friends, or a feeling that you cannot cope with the demands placed upon you.

Stress can be integral to our lives, but understanding the difference between positive and negative stress is critical to managing our well-being. Positive stress can be seen as a motivating force, while negative stress can be overwhelming and lead to physical and emotional exhaustion. We need to treat our stress according to the kinds of emotions they elicit. Positive stress must be treated as a source of motivation, whereas negative stress must be avoided and taken care of accordingly.

Jay had experienced a proper amount of eustress, while Dan had severe distress. Thus, Jay would be more likely to get benefits through his stress, while Dan suffered due to his.

It is essential to recognize the sources of stress in your life and find ways to manage them. Only by effectively recognizing negative stress can you deal with it accordingly. This could include taking regular breaks, developing a support system, and engaging in activities that bring a sense of relaxation.

Stress Management

Stress management is an essential life skill that everyone must learn and practice to lead a healthy and prosperous life. It is the ability to recognize and handle life's stressors and stay calm and focused in chaotic or stressful situations. Stress management is not the same as stress reduction, which entails getting rid of the causes of stress. Stress can manifest as physical, mental, and emotional strain, originating from various sources such as work, relationships, finances, and overwhelming life events. Due to the vast array of possible sources, it is important to identify and address the source of your stress in the first place. Once identified, you can take appropriate measures to curb this source and deal with your stress. This process is called stress management.

Stress management is an integral part of maintaining good physical and mental health. Research has found that prolonged stress can lead to physical and psychological problems, ranging from headaches and anxiety to depression and heart disease. It is important to recognize the signs of stress and take steps to manage it before it affects our health. This can be done through various methods, such as relaxation techniques, physical exercise, and lifestyle changes.

Understanding the sources of your stress is the first step in effective stress management. This can be done through journaling or talking to a therapist. Once the sources of stress are identified, strategies and techniques can be implemented to help reduce and manage it. This may include incorporating relaxation techniques, engaging in regular physical exercise, practicing effective time management, and making relevant lifestyle adjustments.

It is important to remember that stress is a normal part of life, and can't always be avoided. However, with effective stress management, it can be managed and limited to healthy levels. It is essential to prioritize your mental and physical health and make time to relax and unwind. With the right strategies in place, stress can be managed and controlled.

Tips on How to Create a Better Balance

There's no doubt that work pressure and the workload dumped on employees have increased in recent years. One has to work hard to keep their job. But does that mean we should have no life other than our job? Definitely not. Knowing how to balance personal and professional life is the key to solving the issue.

Work frequently takes priority over all other aspects of our existence. We may be tempted to put our well-being last to achieve professional success. However, striking a healthy balance between work and life—also known as work-life integration—is essential to enhancing our physical, emotional, and mental health and even our career.

Know how to differentiate your priorities. Always putting work above everything else will affect your personal relationships. Similarly, always prioritizing your home life over work may affect your professional life. Everything needs its own time. When you are at home, keep your work life aside, and spend some quality time with your family. If needed, go on a vacation and try to relax. Here are some tips for creating a better balance between work and personal life.

There is No Perfect 50-50 Balance

It is unrealistic to believe there is a perfect 50/50 work-life balance. The reality is that life is full of ups and downs, and work-life balance is constantly shifting. The idea of a perfect work-life balance is a myth, as it is hard to have a perfectly balanced schedule all the time. Everyone has to make compromises in life to make it work.

Find a middle ground between your professional and personal life. It's important to know which sacrifices are worth making. Though it isn't an easy task to accomplish, it will be worth it.

There will be days when work demands more of your time, while on other days, family and personal needs take priority. Hence, it is important to remember that it is okay to have slight imbalances in your work-life balance and that it is not a sign of failure. It is perfectly acceptable to prioritize one over the other when need be as long as you are mindful of what is important to you and ensure that each aspect of your life is getting the attention it needs.

Moreover, sustainability is key to maintaining a healthy work-life balance. Even if a sacrifice is worth it, you need to ensure that your physical, mental, and emotional well-being can handle it. You should be aware of your needs and limits to ensure you are not overwhelmed or burnt out. Taking time to relax and recharge is essential to staying focused and productive.

Find a Job You Love

In the book, 'No Man Is an Island', the author, Thomas Merton, says, "Who is willing to be satisfied with a job that expresses all his limitations? He will accept such work only as a "means of livelihood" while he waits to discover his "true vocation." The world is full of unsuccessful businessmen who still secretly believe they were meant to be artists or writers or actors in the movies."

Finding a job you love can be a daunting task. It takes patience, research, and experimentation to find the right fit. But if you take the time to figure out your passion, you can find a personally and professionally rewarding job.

Not everyone knows what their calling is, and that's completely normal and completely okay. Sometimes you have to be in the wrong place to know what's right for you. If you are unsure about what could be right for you, then let's analyze it step-by-step.

Begin by evaluating your skills and interests. Reflect on what you excel at and what genuinely brings you joy. Compile a list of potential career paths that align with your strengths. However, being realistic is important every step of the way. Take into consideration the job market and how your skills fit into it. It's important to be realistic about the job opportunities available.

Next, research the industries and companies that fit your interests. Read job descriptions and company profiles to determine if the roles and environments are a good fit for you. Leverage your professional network to gather insights and gain an insider's perspective on different organizations.

Explore avenues to gain practical experience in your desired field. Enroll in relevant classes, seek out volunteering opportunities, or secure an internship to acquire firsthand knowledge of the industry. This hands-on experience will provide valuable insights into the nature of the work and assist in determining if it aligns with your aspirations.

Finally, apply for jobs that fit your qualifications and interests. Don't be afraid to take risks and apply for jobs outside your comfort zone. You never know what opportunities might be waiting for you.

Finding a job that brings you fulfillment and satisfaction is indeed achievable. It requires dedication and perseverance, but the rewards are invaluable.

Prioritize Your Health

In every aspect of life, we face two types of barriers. One is physical health and the second is mental health. Both are directly linked - if one fails, the other is affected equally, if not more. Thus, they both are the utmost important factors in determining whether you lead a content life.

Health is the most critical aspect of life and should be prioritized to maintain a good work-life balance. Being productive and successful in life is almost impossible if you're not healthy. Having a healthy lifestyle is not only beneficial to overall well-being but also helps in maintaining a healthy work-life balance.

According to WHO, health is a fundamental human right which is of utmost importance for human dignity, social justice, and sustainable development.

Maintaining a healthy lifestyle includes eating a balanced diet, getting enough sleep, and exercising regularly. Eating a balanced diet helps provide the body with all the necessary vitamins, minerals, and other essential nutrients required for growth and development. Getting enough sleep helps restore energy levels and helps the body stay active and alert. Exercising regularly helps build immunity, improve overall physical fitness, and provide a sense of mental and emotional balance. These practices collectively foster a healthy lifestyle, leading to reduced stress levels and improved productivity.

Don't Fear Unplugging

When an electrical outlet is overheating or malfunctioning, you wisely remove all plugs to prevent damage. Similarly, when you find yourself overworked and exhausted, you need to unplug from your hectic life and start making time for yourself. You need to prioritize your well-being.

The notion of unplugging and taking a break from the hustle and bustle of everyday life can seem daunting, but maintaining a healthy work-life balance is essential. When we unplug, it can feel like we are disconnecting from our productivity and hindering our potential for success. However, on the contrary, taking breaks and stepping away can actually be beneficial in the long run, as it allows us to rejuvenate ourselves and increase our productivity and focus.

Feeling anxious when unplugging and taking a break is normal. We may have concerns about our work suffering or missing out on important updates. However, taking some time off can be beneficial in the long run. Unplugging allows us to step back and gain a fresh perspective on our work and life. We can assess our progress and analyze which aspects of our lifestyle are working out and which aren't. This will help us decide what changes we need to make to improve our work-life balance. It also provides an opportunity to escape the fast-paced routine and find solace in moments of tranquility.

Taking a break from work also allows us to focus on our physical and mental health, along with giving us time to spend with our loved ones. We can use this time to exercise, enjoy some hobbies, and spend time with our friends or family. It can also be a great way to boost our creativity and productivity. Giving ourselves a break makes us more likely to return to work feeling refreshed and motivated.

Rather than fearing unplugging, it is important to embrace it as a means to improve our work-life balance and reduce stress. It is a great way to improve our work-life balance and reduce stress. Taking a break from work can help us reconnect with our passions, focus on our physical and mental health, and gain perspective on our life and career. Unplugging can be a positive and rewarding experience if we take the time to enjoy it. So, instead of fearing unplugging, let us embrace it and savor the benefits of a healthier and more balanced lifestyle.

Create Time for Yourself and Your Loved Ones

Creating time for yourself and your loved ones is essential to maintaining a healthy work-life balance. Amidst the hustle and bustle of daily life, it is easy to overlook the importance of allocating time for the people and activities that deserve our attention. It's crucial to prioritize your work-life balance if you want make sure you're making the most of your time.

A key component in prioritizing your work-life balance is to make a plan. Set aside time each week to focus on yourself and your loved ones. This could include exercising, reading, spending time with family and friends, or taking work breaks. When planning these activities, make sure that they don't turn into chores. These activities must hold personal meaning, thus allowing you to form memories with your loved ones, and they must rejuvenate you and leave you ready to work.

When it comes to taking time out for yourself and loved ones, ensuring you are getting enough rest and relaxation is crucial. Taking breaks from work and dedicating time for yourself and loved ones can help maintain a healthy work-life balance. Allowing oneself to take time off for relaxation, unwinding, and enjoying the company of loved ones contributes to building relationships and strengthening bonds.

Examining Your Work-Life Balance

You know you are tired from the daily hustle and bustle of your life. You know work has started to exhaust you. And you know that you need a long-needed vacation. But have you ever noticed *which of your habits exactly* are exhausting you? If not, here are a few things to think about.

- Do you respond to any emails or texts immediately after receiving them post-work hours?

- How much time are you spending on work as compared to with your loved ones?

- Do you feel guilty about not checking your emails or devices for a while?

- Are you hesitant about taking a few days off for no reason?

- Have you experienced any body aches or migraines in the last few weeks?

Did you answer these questions honestly? And if you did, did you gain a bit more clarity about the status of your work-life balance?

Find and Set Your "End Goal"

Whether you are an entrepreneur, a student, or an employee, you can feel overwhelmed and exhausted by the demands of your job or lifestyle. Setting an end goal is absolutely crucial if you want to overcome burnout.

Start by reflecting on what you value most in life and what you want to achieve. Keeping this as well as your mental and physical well-being in mind, think about the areas of your life that you want to prioritize and the kind of lifestyle you want to lead. Think about the career path you'd like to take and how you can progress toward it. A clear end goal provides focus, purpose, and motivation. Thinking about all of these aspects beforehand gives you a fair idea of what you need to do.

Create a plan of action to stay on track. Break it down into smaller steps and establish a timeline for reaching each milestone. This helps you stay organized and focused. Additionally, recognize your achievements and reward yourself for completing each step. Just as it is important for your employer to appreciate your efforts, it is important for you to recognize your achievements as well.

Connecting with friends and family or seeking professional help if you feel overwhelmed can reduce stress levels and give you a sense of control over your life.

By finding and setting an end goal and creating a plan of action to reach it, you can take back control and start to overcome burnout. Regular self-care activities and allowing yourself to take breaks when needed will also help you stay motivated and energized. If you persevere with dedication and commitment, you can achieve your end goal and experience greater positivity and fulfillment in life.

Now that our mind is properly set to reach a goal that is worth it to us, we need to address any obstacles or hindrances to reaching that goal. Let's set some non-negotiable boundaries in the next chapter.

Chapter 5

Drawing the Line in the Sand

"What you allow is what will continue."
~ Unknown

D AVID HAD ALWAYS BEEN a people pleaser, finding it difficult to say no to his boss or coworkers. He'd had the same problem since he was in school. He felt like he had to be constantly available and accommodating, even at the expense of his own time and energy.

Initially, David's willingness to take on extra work and assist his colleagues was seen as a positive trait. His dedication earned him praise from his boss, and his coworkers relied on him to handle their workload when they struggled.

However, as time passed, David began to feel increasingly overwhelmed and overworked. His responsibilities kept growing, and his workload seemed to expand daily. He was staying late at the office and bringing work home with him and experiencing mounting stress each week. All of this, and yet, his pay remained the same.

One day, David's boss asked him to take on yet another project. David felt a sinking feeling in his heart as he knew that he simply couldn't take on any more work without sacrificing his own well-being.

In the past, David would have unquestioningly agreed to take on the project. But this time, something within him sparked. A small voice urged him to stand up for himself and say no.

Taking a deep breath, David met his boss's gaze and firmly stated. "I'm sorry, but I can't take on this project right now," he said firmly. "I already have a lot on my plate, and I don't want to compromise the quality of my work or my own well-being by taking on too much."

His boss looked surprised, but to David's relief, he didn't insist further. It wasn't easy for David to learn to say no. He had to confront his own fears of disappointing others and of being seen as unhelpful or lazy.

With time, David learned that saying no wasn't a sign of weakness but rather an act of strength and self-care. While it wasn't always easy, it felt good to have the courage to stand up for himself and to prioritize his own needs, even in the face of pressure from others.

Setting workplace boundaries is an integral part of maintaining a healthy work-life balance. Without proper boundaries, burnout, stress, and decreased job satisfaction can ensue, as in David's case. Boundaries help you manage your workload, focus on essential tasks and avoid being overwhelmed.

By setting boundaries at your workplace, you establish a better understanding of expectations from your employers. It also allows you to be more productive and efficient, reducing your risk of burnout and stress.

For effective boundary establishment and enforcement, employers should encourage open communication, establish clear expectations, and be responsive to employee needs and concerns. Feedback and guidance should be provided when necessary.

This chapter will examine ways to effectively communicate our boundaries to our employer and increase our chances of a favorable outcome. We will also address possible boundaries you can set if you work from home.

How a Lack of Boundaries Can Lead to Burnout

David had finally found it in himself to say "No" to others. But what if he hadn't? Or what if after he had said "no", his boss forced the project on him anyway? Would David still have the courage to say "No" to anyone else in the future? How do you think he would've turned out then?

Having to say, 'No' in situations where you are uncomfortable or disinterested can be quite daunting. Especially when the person you have to say "no" 'is closely related to you, or is a leader at your workplace. It could be disadvantageous when you lack boundaries as it can affect your physical and mental health. There is also the chance of being taken advantage of when you lack clear boundaries.

Without proper boundaries, people are more likely to take on more work than they can handle. This can lead to feeling overwhelmed, and a sense of being unable to meet the demands of their job. Working long hours and not taking the time to rest or take a break can add to the feeling of burnout. It can be challenging to set boundaries when trying to please everyone around you, but it is essential to ensure you are not taking on too much. David, as a people's pleaser, was facing this issue.

Another factor that can lead to burnout is not having any control over your work. It is essential to have some control over your work and to be able to voice your opinion. Feeling like you are not heard, or your views are ignored can lead to frustration and helplessness. This can cause increased stress levels and can eventually lead to burnout. If David's boss had given him the project, he most likely would've experienced severe burnout, as well as a stronger inability to refuse others.

As Warren Buffett once said, "*The difference between successful people and really successful people is that really successful people say 'No' to almost everything.*" So, have the courage to say "No" to a colleague who asks you to take up their work if your plate is already full. Say 'No' to your boss, if they ask you to do something that goes beyond your values.

Furthermore, if negative people or negative situations constantly surround you, it can lead to feelings of stress and exhaustion. This can interfere with your ability to cope and can contribute to burnout. Removing yourself from negative people and situations is essential to maintain mental and emotional health.

Taking care of your physical health by eating well, exercising, and taking time to relax and practice self-care, can all help to prevent burnout. These activities can help reduce stress levels and help you maintain a healthy balance. Here we will examine a variety of ways in which we can set physical, emotional, and mental boundaries.

Physical Boundaries

Would you be okay with a colleague or a boss touching you casually as friends, especially if you're not all that friendly with them? Or with someone taking your things from your desk without your permission? Or worse, someone accessing your online accounts to look for something or go through your search history? I'll assume, not. Well, this would be the result, if you do not set personal boundaries at your workplace.

Physical boundary, in general, is a protective shield that keeps you safe from any unwanted touch, violation of your personal space, or denial of your physical needs. It also includes not extending your work hours, not sacrificing your breaks, and maintaining proper health. We should be clear about our needs and preferences at work, so as to not let someone cross our physical boundary.

Maintaining physical boundaries at work is important to maintaining a healthy career and preventing burnout and stress. As such, it is essential to understand and practice these boundaries to ensure a healthy and productive work environment.

One fundamental physical boundary is maintaining a respectful distance between colleagues, particularly in an office setting. This allows for privacy and respect. In addition, it is vital to maintain a certain level of professionalism by avoiding physical contact. This includes forbidding, limiting, and refraining from physical touch with colleagues, which can create discomfort and hostility in certain individuals.

Another critical physical boundary is in regard to personal items. Keeping personal items out of the workplace is essential, as these can be distracting and make the workspace feel less professional. Additionally, it is important to respect the personal items of others and vice versa, such as not touching your personal things or taking them without your permission.

Finally, physical boundaries extend to technology and the internet. Awareness about technology boundaries at work is vital, as it helps prevent the invasion of other people's privacy.

Surprisingly, a survey conducted by 'The New York Times' in 2020, showed that harassment at work continued even while working from home. Some employees had taken advantage of the internet to send inappropriate messages or images, and even made unwanted advances.

So, being aware of the boundaries of using the internet at work is crucial. This includes refraining from using the internet for personal use, and limiting the time spent online. This supports a productive work environment and demonstrates respect for privacy.

Physical boundaries are essential to creating a healthy and productive work environment. Understanding and practicing these boundaries helps to prevent burnout and stress, as well as maintain a sense of professionalism and respect.

Emotional Boundaries

Have you ever been in a position where you tried to seek help from your colleague or friend or even a family member but instead of receiving empathy, you were shunned? Do you often say "yes" solely to please others or feel guilty when you say "No"? Do you feel disrespected by your boss or colleagues, but are afraid to stand up for yourself? These could be signs of not having emotional boundaries set up.

It is also important to set boundaries around how work affects emotions. For example, it is essential to recognize when emotions are hindering your productivity and to then deal with them accordingly. Additionally, setting boundaries around how feelings are discussed in the workplace is necessary. Recognizing that everyone has different experiences and respecting those experiences in the workplace is essential. Creating a space for positive emotion management and regulation is crucial for productivity.

Finally, setting boundaries around how emotional support is provided at work is important. It is important to recognize when emotional support is needed and seek appropriate resources when necessary. This can create a supportive work environment and prevent burnout and stress.

Mental Boundaries

While physical boundaries protect us from external conflicts, mental boundaries are set up to protect us from internal conflicts. We need to set up mental boundaries to keep us safe from our own thoughts, feelings, and beliefs.

Creating mental boundaries at work involves:

- Understanding what is expected of you.

- Understanding your limits.

- Creating a plan to manage the expectations of others.

The first step to setting up mental boundaries at work is understanding the scope of your job. Clarify the goals, objectives, and expected tasks of your role. Create a plan to manage your workload, including a realistic timeline and organizational strategies. This prevents burnout and stress by avoiding excessive work.

The second step is recognizing your limits. Understand your most productive times and plan accordingly. If mornings are when you experience peak productivity, prioritize important tasks during that time. By understanding your limits, you can avoid an overwhelming workload and prevent burnout and stress.

The third step in setting mental boundaries at work is to create a plan for managing the expectations of others. This plan should include strategies for setting boundaries, such as politely declining requests you cannot fulfill and requesting reasonable extensions on deadlines when necessary. By creating such a plan, you can maintain a manageable workload and prevent becoming overwhelmed by job demands.

Ways to Set Healthy Boundaries at Work

Henry Cloud, a psychologist and author, once said, "*Boundaries define us. They define what is me and what is not me. A boundary shows me where I end and someone else begins, leading me to a sense of ownership. Knowing what I am to own and take responsibility for gives me freedom.*"

Boundaries are a great thing, but unfortunately, setting them can be difficult for some. It's normal to feel anxious or nervous about setting boundaries at work because we are concerned that we will be viewed as less accessible, less productive, undedicated, or as not being a team player. It's essential to recognize that you are only human and have limitations like everyone else.

Let's go over a few points about how to establish appropriate boundaries at work.

Finding Your Personal Values

Before you can set your boundaries, you need to know your personal values. Finding your values is essential to living a fulfilled and meaningful life. Personal values are things that you believe are essential to both your life and work. They influence your decisions and priorities, and have an impact on your personality. Knowing what is important to you and making decisions based on these values can help you make better decisions, manage stress, and prevent burnout. It can also help you set boundaries and prioritize your work as you seek to live a life that aligns with your beliefs and ideals.

The first step to finding your personal values is to reflect on what makes you feel fulfilled. What are your passions? What values guide your actions? Delve deep into what makes you feel alive. Once you have recognized your core values, you can take steps to live in alignment with them.

For instance, if one of your core values is self-care, you can make sure that you prioritize taking time for yourself and engaging in activities that help you relax and find balance. This could include making time for exercise, going for walks, or taking a break from work. Similarly, if one of your values is having meaningful relationships, you can actively seek out opportunities to connect with people in meaningful ways.

You can also create a list of your values and refer to it whenever you are faced with a difficult decision or a challenging situation. When you feel overwhelmed, step back and ask yourself which of your values is most relevant to the current situation. This will aid in determining the best course of action that aligns with your beliefs.

When determining your personal values, it's essential to keep some things in mind, such as being honest with yourself and respecting your feelings. Finding your personal values is a journey. It requires reflection, and it can take time to identify what is important to you and start making decisions that align with these values. But it is worth the time and the effort, as it can help you create a more meaningful life and prevent burnout by setting boundaries and making conscious decisions about how to spend your time and energy.

Be Honest With Yourself

It is essential to be honest with oneself when setting boundaries. Honesty is the foundation of creating boundaries that are to be respected and followed.

Oscar Wilde once said, "*The truth is rarely pure and never simple.*" Our honesty with ourselves has a huge impact on our life. It can be tough to be honest while setting our boundaries, but it will be worth it.

When setting boundaries, it is essential to be honest about what you are capable of and feel comfortable with. It is easy to overcommit or feel like you should be able to do more than you can. However, a failure to be honest here can lead you to situations where you end up feeling overwhelmed or facing burnout. Therefore, it is crucial to be honest about how much work and commitment you can handle and ensure that your boundaries reflect these limits.

Another vital aspect of being honest when setting boundaries is being honest about your needs. This could be anything from needing time to yourself to taking a break from a particular activity or asking for help. Recognizing your needs and being honest with yourself about them is essential. This can help prevent burnout and ensure that you take care of yourself.

Being honest with oneself is also essential when reflecting on your set boundaries and determining whether or not they are working. Boundaries are subject to change based on how you grow as a human being as well as your surroundings. Only if you are honest with yourself can you identify when your boundaries are not respected or need to be adjusted. This ensures the maintenance of effective boundaries and a healthy work-life balance.

Respect Your Feelings

Confucius, a Chinese Philosopher, said, "*Respect yourself and others will respect you.*" It is important to respect ourselves and our feelings to become more self-aware.

Respecting your feelings when determining personal values is critical to success in life. It is essential to take the time to be mindful of how your actions and decisions are making you feel. When you feel overwhelmed or anxious at work, it is essential to take a step back and determine what is causing you to feel that way. Only when you analyze the situation can you determine what steps you need to take in order to align your work with your values.

When determining your values, it is vital to acknowledge the feelings that come up when making decisions. This could be anything from feeling empowered by a particular project to feeling exhausted by the amount of work you have been given. It is essential to take the time to listen to your own feelings and to think about how they are affecting your overall lifestyle. It is essential to take care of your own feelings if you want to lead a fulfilling life. To honor your feelings, you need to recognize them first, and then you can ensure that your work aligns with your personal values.

Having a solid understanding of your values is essential to long-term success. This means taking the time to understand what makes you tick and to determine what values are important to you. It also means respecting your feelings when making decisions, whether at work or in your personal life. Respect for your feelings and an understanding of your personal values can ensure that you are living your life in a way that aligns with your goals.

Make Sure Everything Is In Alignment

It becomes easier to set the parameters of your boundaries once you have defined your personal values. Take the time to assess your current work and lifestyle. What parts of your lifestyle are working for you right now and which ones are not? Be sure to evaluate your lifestyle in all three aspects: physical, mental, and emotional. Keep track of your thoughts on paper or electronically. This will help you organize your thoughts and strategically reach your goals. Before you begin enforcing your boundaries, it is essential to note that they do not infract upon the duties and responsibilities of your job requirement.

Examine the Assignment

When you're assigned a task or a project at your workplace, ensure the assignment is reasonable before discussing it with your management or fellow employee. Don't take up tasks that you have no understanding about or give a deadline before analyzing even the prerequisites of the task just to impress your employer.

Similarly, if your boss offers you a challenging task, instead of assuming it's beyond your scope right away, ask them for further resources so you can learn how to approach it. If you choose to accept a challenge, you may just end up being surprised by what you're capable of. If you're wondering whether a request falls under the purview of your job responsibilities, evaluate your job description and consider how similar the task is to your other obligations. You can also ask your team members if the requirements are typical for a working environment. In any case, it's crucial to have a dialogue with your manager if their request breaches one of your personal or professional limits.

Ideas to Get You Started

We've discussed how messed up today's work-life balance is. We've also talked about some ways to improve the situation. Those were the bigger issues. However, even the smallest of habits can lead to imbalances in life. Below are additional ways to keep the lines between work and personal values clear and well-defined.

Keep Your Office Computer at Work

In a survey conducted by Robert Half in 2019, it was found that 39 percent of employees had trouble disconnecting themselves from their work, and more often than not worked during their personal time. This could not only hinder their mental and physical well-being but also disrupt their personal relationships.

Try to make it a habit to work exclusively at the office. Also, remove any work-related applications, such as Slack, from your home computer to avoid temptations to work. Don't carry your work home. Leave your work at the workplace.

Restrict the Routes of Communication

Do you utilize email, Slack, Google Chat, and other platforms to communicate with coworkers and business partners? A survey of working professionals revealed that almost half of them believed that having multiple communication channels made them feel less focused and effective.

Rather than monitoring three different email accounts and a million Slack channels, centralizing your communication would be more efficient. Streamlining your communication would help streamline your focus as well. This would entail consolidating all your email accounts and deleting any Slack channels that aren't necessary.

If you shuttle most of your time between various online platforms, you will have little to no time or energy to spend on yourself or with your family. It could lead to extreme levels of stress, addiction to the internet, and it could also cause anxiety or depression. Hence, it is essential to have a work-life balance and reduce your screen time as much as possible.

Recognize Your Workload

In a survey conducted by the American Psychological Association, workload seemed to be one of the major reasons behind feeling burned out. Having an overwhelming workload could lead to stress, anxiety, and depression.

Many people find themselves feeling overwhelmed and stressed by the demands of their job. Analyzing your workload and comprehending its scope, as well as its components, along with the number of responsibilities you can manage daily is critical. Knowing these things can help you set more assertive boundaries for your work obligations and maintain daily productivity. Think about how long it takes to complete jobs or track how many you can finish in a workday. If you are constantly falling behind or working overtime regularly to keep up, it's an indication that it is time to reassess your workload.

Assign duties to others if you are in a position to delegate. Delegating job duties is an essential step to relieving stress in the workplace. When this happens, you must step back and delegate some of your job duties to others. Delegating job duties will give you a more balanced workload, reducing the stress of doing everything yourself.

One Boss Rule

The one-boss rule simply means to report to one boss or one supervisor. Having too many people to report to could cause major confusion and disruptions in your work.

Set limits with those who aren't your immediate supervisor. How frequently has a coworker come by your desk with a "quick question" that takes you over 20 minutes to answer? Although it can be difficult to refuse someone who requests assistance, you should limit non-urgent inquiries to a minimum if you are extremely busy at work. Instead, politely ask them to email you about the problem if it is not urgent so you may address it later.

Keep Your Personal Mode of Communication Private

Do you get unwanted texts such as good morning messages, WhatsApp forwards, or jokes from a colleague with whom you shared your number for work purposes?

Having friendly relationships with colleagues may be a good thing both within and outside work. So, sometimes it makes perfect sense to share your mobile phone number with coworkers. After all, who knows? Perhaps someday, you'll travel together or have a friendship outside of work. However, the lines become slightly blurry when your colleagues text you about work-related matters after hours. Ask coworkers respectfully not to text your cell phone number concerning work unless it's an urgent situation only you can handle. You can also set your mobile to silence notifications after work hours.

How to Talk to Your Manager

Feel free to have a robust discussion with your manager about how you are feeling and what you are going through. Such feelings are not the kind you should keep to yourself. Managers are in an ideal position to provide assistance, lighten workloads, and foster safer work environments for their employees.

Remember David? His boss was considerate and held good relationships with all his employees. So, when David refused to take on another project, he was surprised, but he still agreed to David's request. Realistically, though, it's unlikely that all bosses will be that easily agreeable. Thus, it's always better to be prepared for having a discussion with your boss or manager. When approaching your manager about your new set of boundaries, think positively, and be open to other resolutions your manager proposes.

Assess Your Emotions

Before addressing the issue with your supervisor, give yourself time to digest any dissatisfaction you may feel. You could experience annoyance or discomfort when someone makes an unreasonable demand. Even worse, you might feel insulted or undervalued if your manager assigned you a task that has nothing to do with your job, like performing a personal errand. In situations like these, where your feelings might end up getting the best of you, allowing yourself to cool down before addressing the matter will enable you to approach your manager professionally and respectfully. It can also initiate a productive conversation about the impact of their actions on you.

Prepare in Advance

Feeling emotionally incapable of discussing the matter with your manager is to be expected, especially if you have trouble expressing yourself or suffer from mental fog. But trust me, it's a discussion worth having. If you need help approaching the subject, try outlining your thoughts in a script. Writing down your thoughts and feelings on a piece of paper would help make them feel more solid. By doing this, your confidence in expressing these thoughts and feelings to your manager may be boosted significantly.

Prepare by writing out precisely everything you want to say to your manager. Identify each issue and its possible resolution. When you and your manager have discussed possible solutions, you will be equally concerned about your well-being. It's also acceptable if you cannot come up with solutions as long as you are honest about it.

Since burnout impacts not just you but also your teammates, your newfound goals can promote efficiency and productivity. This makes them beneficial for your team or your organization, and that is how they should be brought up with your manager. —This will also ensure that they are received much more readily and agreeably.

Speak With a Trusted Person

Taking small steps to have a meaningful conversation with your manager is advisable, as it can be an intimidating process. Tell a friend how you're feeling or talk to a dependable coworker to get their feedback before approaching your manager one-on-one. The perspectives you get from these sources can provide you with invaluable information and insight. They might even be willing to role-play the conversation with your manager and offer practical suggestions to improve the chances of a positive outcome.

Lead the Charge

Speaking with your manager about your new changes can be intimidating, especially if you don't usually have friendly or personal conversations with each other regularly. However, it is essential to communicate with your manager directly and promptly to dispel any misunderstandings. Most managers will likely be too busy to have an impromptu meeting with you on the spot, so ask ahead to reserve an hour or so on their calendar at a future date for a private one-on-one discussion. If face-to-face chats with your manager make you nervous, consider writing an email first with an offer to discuss the matter further at a convenient time. This would, in turn, also prepare your manager for the conversation you're about to have with them.

Be Professional and Polite

Being professional and polite when speaking with your manager is essential, especially when discussing such a sensitive topic. Doing so shows that you respect them and are reasonable and willing to be cooperative. Following these simple guidelines will help you to have a successful discussion:

1. Always address your manager by their title and surname.

2. Always wait for your manager to be finished before speaking.

3. Speak clearly and concisely.

4. Always answer questions truthfully and completely.

5. Show respect for your manager by keeping your emotions in check.

Remind Them of Your Job Description

When duties fall outside the jurisdiction of your job description, politely reminding your manager or supervisor may be enough to justify your lack of comfort or ability to dedicate yourself to that particular work. Your manager may accept that their request was unreasonable in light of a good cause and cooperate with you to find a solution. By explaining to your manager why a request is unrealistic, you can start a fruitful discussion about your responsibilities and job description and create a positive precedent for subsequent interactions. Consider giving details on alternate duties that are within your capabilities and limitations when establishing this limit.

For instance:

"I can't commit to picking up your dry cleaning because I believe that my time would be better spent working on the responsibilities related to graphic design included in my job description."

"I'm sorry, but as a junior accountant, my present responsibility already occupies my calendar. However, I'm willing to help with any bookkeeping tasks within my expertise."

"I'm happy to alter my schedule to give this priority more attention, but the earliest I can turn in the assignment is Tuesday to retain the quality."

Be Open-Minded

Managers and, by extension, companies reward "can do" attitudes. So, do not be surprised if your manager seems disappointed in the initial stages of the conversation. Keep your composure and remain calm. To ease the tension, assure your manager that you are willing to work towards finding solutions with him and offer any recommendations that you might have.

You need not compromise your core values but be open to compromising on less critical issues that don't affect you significantly, like offering to work an extra thirty minutes during the weekdays instead of having to come in to work on the weekends. Compromising in the workplace is a crucial factor to success. It is essential to recognize the importance of compromise and be willing to apply the principle when needed.

When you are willing to compromise in some areas, it shows your manager that you are a team player, are open to collaboration, and that you value the opinions of others. This type of attitude is essential in any workplace as it demonstrates that you are invested in the success of the organization, and it can lead to increased respect from your manager. Compromising also helps to spread the workload more evenly, ensuring that tasks are shared fairly among the team.

Before you meet with your manager, brainstorm solutions and develop potential alternatives yourself to demonstrate that you are aware of the ramifications of your boundaries and are prepared to shoulder some of the responsibility.

When You Experience Push Backs

David decided to change his approach to work after refusing that project. He was still friendly with others and tried to help them as best as he could, but he no longer picked up their slacks. His colleagues soon got the hint and stopped trying to pass on their work to him. However, there will always be those who try to get in the way of your change. Some of his colleagues were not happy with his new boundaries and started to cause issues for him.

People at work who are unable to acclimate to the new you may start to push back once you start making these changes. They would rather choose the colleague who always replies to their emails promptly instead of the one who takes a while. If others don't agree with your new work approach, calmly explain why you're acting this way and how it helps you to cope with stress.

If you suffer workplace discrimination because of your changes or if your manager refuses to cooperate with your new boundaries and you feel that your health or safety is in danger, do not hesitate to speak with a human resource personnel or seek outside assistance.

Be Proactive

"The proactive approach is to change from the 'inside-out': to be different, and by being different, to effect positive change in what's out there - I can be more resourceful, I can be more diligent, I can be more creative, I can be more cooperative." - Stephen Covey.

A proactive approach is taking control of a situation rather than waiting for it to play out and then reacting to it. The damage control to be done post a situation crisis can greatly increase stress and workload. When we take a proactive approach instead, it helps us avoid damage and reduce stress. It gives us a sense of responsibility and empowers us with problem-solving abilities.

Rather than expecting others to change their ways, consider being proactive by changing your behavior instead. For example, if discussions with coworkers tend to be negative, gossipy, or make you feel uncomfortable, try finding an alternate place to have your lunch or take your lunch break at a different time than they usually do.

Look for Another Job

Has your boss suddenly become very critical of your work? Or have they suddenly started to point out flaws in your work or taken away your autonomy? Are you excluded from conversations or events you used to be part of? Suddenly being left out of meetings or out of the loop on important decisions could signify that you're not valuable to the team anymore. Increased workload without clear explanations or inadequate guidance and support could further imply intentional efforts to make your job more challenging.

No one wants to think about being fired, but knowing the signs can help you be prepared for the future. By being aware of how your boss treats you and paying attention to any changes in your workload, you can prepare for the possibility of being laid off by keeping your sights open to new job openings. Your state labor and industrial relations department is a good resource for employment opportunities in your area, in addition to online job postings.

Honoring Your Boundaries

It's essential to be consistent with your words and actions at work. This will help to build trust and credibility with your coworkers, while also ensuring that the work you do is effective and efficient. If you are inconsistent, your coworkers may not believe what you say or do is worth paying attention to. For example, if you say you are unreachable on weekends but respond to their texts, emails, or calls during those times, then your boundaries become inconsequential or negotiable to them.

When you set boundaries and honor them, you show your employers and colleagues that you respect your time and energy and so they should too. This can also help you feel empowered and in control of your life.

By honoring your boundaries, you can prioritize the important things and ensure that you are not overburdening yourself with too much work. It is important to remember that boundaries are not just about saying "no" to specific tasks but also about saying "yes" to the things that are important to you. Having appropriate boundaries allows you to focus on the tasks you are most passionate about and takes care of your needs.

When setting boundaries in the workplace, it is essential to be flexible and open to change. This will help ensure that your boundaries are realistic and achievable. It is also important to remember that boundaries are not set in stone. You can adjust and modify your boundaries according to your needs.

By honoring your boundaries in the workplace, you will be able to prioritize your tasks and take care of your needs better, which will help reduce your stress and burnout levels. Setting and honoring boundaries can also help you feel empowered and in control of your life.

Setting Boundaries When You Work From Home

Remember Mark? His work-life balance had been disturbed due to online work from home. Unfortunately, it was a situation he could've avoided.

Working from home has become increasingly popular, with remote job opportunities becoming increasingly available. While there are plenty of advantages to this arrangement, there are also some important considerations that need to be taken into account. Setting boundaries when working from home is essential to ensure that you can capitalize on the opportunity instead of letting it adversely impact your life.

Having clearly defined boundaries when working from home is vital to maintaining a healthy work-life balance. Working from home can easily blur the lines between home and work if you don't set appropriate boundaries, leading to burnout and stress. Setting boundaries helps establish clear expectations for yourself and those around you. It can help to ensure that you aren't constantly available at your employer's whim, even when working from home. Setting boundaries when working from home also means being able to separate your work from your personal life. Working from home can make it difficult to switch off, as you are constantly surrounded by reminders of work rather than having a physical separation between home and work. Boundaries can ensure that you're able to dedicate time to other activities and take regular breaks.

Finally, having boundaries when working from home can help create a more organized, productive work environment. Having clear expectations and schedules can ensure that you are more effective and can focus on the task at hand. It can also create a healthy routine and make planning and taking on additional duties easier.

Have a Dedicated Work Space

Maintaining a work-life balance is all about your mindset. Working from home doesn't mean that you make your entire home your workplace, it means setting up a dedicated workspace inside your home that doesn't overlap with your personal life. Granted, not everyone has an extra room to dedicate to their home office. However, even if you live in a small apartment, you can still get creative. Set up a location for your work, ideally somewhere calm and free from interruptions. Find a corner in your home that you can convert into a workspace. Set up a partition wall, curtains, or a shoji screen to separate your living space from your workspace. This is going to act as your office now.

Another benefit to having a dedicated workspace is that it helps your brain to switch to work mode more readily and decisively.

Dress for Work

One of the perks of working from home, at least for some, is having the freedom to work in their sweatpants. As comfortable as that may sound, you may wonder, "Will dressing up for work make any difference?" It does. Getting dressed for work (including brushing your teeth and combing your hair) increases your work productivity. It also helps you mentally transition from home to work life and vice versa. If you are asked to give an online presentation or have a meeting with a client, dressing professionally will leave a good impression on them. It also increases your self-confidence and draws positive attention. Your dressing has a huge and powerful impact on how others perceive you, and more importantly how you perceive yourself. Even if you have no scheduled videoconferencing meeting or work alone, it is still important to dress for work.

Set a Regular and Realistic Work Schedule

Setting a regular work schedule and sticking to it will prevent you from working longer than desired and makes it easier for you to schedule leisure time with family and friends. Observing an end time can be just as crucial as a start time. Schedule your start, lunch, break, and end hours. It's equally important to set a regular lunch period regardless of how focused you are on your work. Having a set lunch period is crucial to regulating your body's natural clock and, ultimately, your overall health.

A realistic work schedule could help reduce stress, improve your work-life balance, and prevent you from taking up extra work and pressurizing yourself to complete it. When you set a specific deadline, you can dedicate your time to each task, and know how well and how soon you can deliver your task.

Make Sure to Have a Break

It's best to take frequent breaks to rejuvenate yourself, which would significantly increase your productivity. Your health and concentration can be improved by taking a 5-minute break from your screen every hour. Do not feel that you must constantly be staring at your computer to demonstrate that you are working. You would take regular breaks if you worked in an office, and working from home is no different.

According to William S. Helton, Professor of Human Factors and Applied Cognition at George Mason University, taking breaks can improve our attention.

Working continuously without breaks could cause us to lose focus and lead to a lack of motivation. Effectively scheduled breaks between work hours allow us to focus on our work with a fresh mind. It is essential for both physical and mental health.

Widen Your Association

When we expand our network of contacts within and outside our work, it serves us a lot of benefits. It helps us improve our performance, widen our career opportunities, and it also increases our creativity and innovation.

You shouldn't spend the entire day in silence just because you work from home. Colleagues can still be reached via voice or video calls. Join a group (online or offline) related to your work where people collaborate weekly or on a regular basis. If feasible, join your meetings a few minutes early and try to engage in conversations with your colleagues. Everyone should check in with one another since this would benefit the health of everyone involved.

A report by the Harvard Business School called 'The Value of Belonging at Work,' found that belonging to a workplace not only benefited the employees but it also benefited the company. In this report, it was also found that high belonging resulted in a 56 percent increase in job performance, a 50 percent drop in turnover risks, and a 75 percent reduction in sick days.

Ban Distractions

It is very easy to get distracted when working from home - your dishes need to be washed, you need to put in a load of laundry, give mom a "quick" call, etc. Sometimes, "just a few minutes of social media" turns into hours, and before you know it, two hours have passed, and you still need to turn on your computer.

Being addicted to social media is one of the major distractions that disrupt our work. You'd be surprised to know that, based on a study conducted by the University of California, Irvine, it takes an average of 23 minutes and 15 seconds to refocus when you get distracted.

Limit unnecessary distractions by silencing your cell phone, closing tabs that are not work-related, and limiting the number of times you check your emails to once or twice a day. Speaking of silencing your phone, here's a piece of trivia for you - how many times a day do you think the average smartphone user unlocks his phone? According to a study of 150,000 participants, the answer is....(drumroll)....110 times a day! Unsurprisingly, according to Nir Eyal, "79% of smartphone users check their phone within 15 minutes of waking up".

Clock Out

Do you often take your work home? Do you spend late nights or early mornings holed up at work? Do you check work emails even while you're spending time with family or friends? Then you are probably a workaholic. Being a workaholic strains your personal relations, and also causes stress and anxiety.

Clocking out at the right time when working from home is critical to maintaining a healthy work-life balance. It can help to reduce stress, promote productivity, and increase motivation. Establishing clear boundaries between work and home life is vital to achieving success and maintaining a healthy lifestyle.

One of the benefits of clocking out is that it helps to maintain productivity. Knowing you have a set time to finish work can motivate you to get the job done quickly and efficiently. It also helps to reduce procrastination, as you can focus on the tasks that need to be done instead of getting distracted by other activities.

Another benefit of clocking out is that it increases motivation. When you have a suitable end time to your workday, it can provide a sense of accomplishment, driving you to work harder and be more productive. Knowing that you will clock out at the end of the day, at a time that allows you to have time to yourself afterward, will help keep you motivated and ensure that you reach your goals.

Set Agreements

The most complicated boundary involves your family and coworkers because it depends on both your and their participation. You'll need to establish clear guidelines for yourself and for those around you while working remotely. It's all too common for others to think that you are available at any given moment when you tell them that you work from home.

Respect and collaboration are the goals of boundaries. Inform your family and colleagues of your availability with 100 percent honesty. Your family and coworkers will respect you and your time because of these boundaries. Your family ought to treat your working hours with the same respect as they would if you were working at an employer's office. You may make a sign to let people know when you're available and when you are not, such as leaving the door open or putting up a "Do Not Disturb" or "In A Meeting" sign to indicate that they shouldn't disturb your working hours.

Time for a Change

Time is a funny thing. The paradoxical truth of time is beyond our understanding. Remember how, as a kid, we would sit in our classroom waiting for the day to end, but it would keep on dragging slower every second. Yet, when we would spend our weekends having fun, it would always end sooner than we wished for it to. Time flies when you need it to stay, but it crawls slower than a turtle when you want it to pass. People say, time heals all wounds, but does time wait for us?

Time management is an integral part of leading a successful life. We all have the same 24 hours daily, but how we use them makes all the difference. Without proper time management, it can be all too easy to get overwhelmed with stress and suffer from burnout. Though it may be quite daunting to manage control over time, through proper time management, we can accomplish our goals and manage our physical and mental health at the same time.

Time management is more than making a to-do list and crossing off items. It's about prioritizing tasks and using your time more efficiently. When you have a certain deadline to meet your tasks, you begin to work efficiently and finish it sooner, which boosts your confidence and motivates you to achieve more. Taking a step back and assessing how you're spending your time is a challenging task, but it is absolutely essential to maximizing productivity.

Taking the time to plan and manage your days can help you stay focused and organized. You'll be able to track your tasks and understand better what needs to be done and when. When you have a plan for your days, it's easier to stay on task and avoid the urge to give in to procrastination.

As Steve Jobs, a co-founder of Apple Inc, said, "*Your time is limited, so don't waste it living someone else's life. Don't be trapped by dogma— which is living with the results of other people's thinking. Don't let the noise of others' opinions drown out your inner voice. And most important, have the courage to follow your heart and intuition.*"

Know Your Limitations

On January 19, 2023, Jacinda Arden, the former Prime Minister of New Zealand, announced her resignation. Do you know why? Well, as per her statement, "I know what this job takes, and I know that I no longer have enough in the tank to do it justice." Even though she didn't specifically mention the word "burnout," her statement is believed to be describing it as such.

Knowing your limitations at work is easier said than done and requires a lot of humility. Being ambitious can be rewarding when you have met your goal, but knowing when to draw the line is essential. Trying to meet unrealistic targets can be a source of immense stress and will frequently lead to burnout. Understanding what kind of workload is manageable and what is too much for you is essential.

Limitations can be challenging to recognize, especially if you are a go-getter. People often underestimate their workload and overestimate their abilities. Stress and burnout can easily creep in when you take on more than you can handle. Understanding your capacity limits is crucial to maintaining a healthy work-life balance.

Equally important is recognizing your limitations when it comes to skill. If there are tasks that you don't have the necessary skills for, then it's best to be honest and not take them on. Trying to take on a task without having the required skills or trying to wing it can cause more harm than good. It's not always easy to know when to draw the line, and saying "no" can be difficult. But if you want to avoid burnout and unnecessary negative stress, working within your limitations is paramount.

Track Your Interruptions

Have you noticed yourself wanting to look at your phone for any notifications or emails while you are working? Or do you have a colleague who chats your ear off, taking away your time from doing your work? Well, paying heed to needless notifications from social media and not having the heart to inform your colleague that you are busy with your work are the kinds of interruptions that not only disrupt your focus but also cause a setback in your workflow.

Interruptions in the workplace can cause significant disruptions to work-flow, leading to decreased productivity, and increased stress and work-load. Interruptions can take many forms, such as phone calls, emails, meetings, and conversations. These can significantly impact time man-agement, as you are taken away from your primary tasks to deal with the interruption. The sudden shifts in focus are disruptive and stressful as you try to finish the task at hand while trying to remember where you left off when you were disrupted.

Why not take the time to map out every interruption, every distraction, and every unexpected shift in your workload? Tracking your interrup-tions will help you identify your top distractions and think of ways to dampen these distractions or prevent them from occurring entirely.

Set Priorities

There is a Russian proverb that says, "If you chase two rabbits, you will not catch either one." It means that when you try to run after two or more things, wanting to accomplish them all at the same time, you will most likely end up succeeding in none. Instead, prioritize which of your goals needs your attention first, and then try to achieve that before moving on to the next one.

Prioritizing tasks is a vital part of managing time and workload effective-ly. The first step to prioritizing tasks is to list all the tasks at hand. This list should include all the tasks that need to be completed, regardless of their size. Once the list is created, the next step is to assess each task based on the time and effort required to complete it and its level of importance.

After prioritizing the tasks, it is important to break them down into smaller, more manageable tasks. It is also important to acknowledge that not all tasks will be completed in the same amount of time, and therefore it is essential to be flexible with the timeline for completing tasks.

Plan Your Schedule in Advance

Napoleon Hill once said, "*Plan your work, and work your plan.*" When we prepare in advance for all the criteria that needs to be met for the upcoming week or the next day, it gives us a sense of responsibility and control of time. We relieve a lot of our stress when we know what tasks are to be done and when they need to be done.

Some individuals spend their Sunday evening or Monday morning planning their schedule for the following week. Others plan the next day before signing off at the end of each day. Whichever system you choose, there is no right or wrong time to plan your schedule. Your main objective is to figure out how to dedicate your time in a way that works best for you.

Tune in to Your Ultradian Rhythm

What is 'Ultradian rhythm'? The term refers to cyclic periods of rest and activity of the brain between sleep and the conscious state in human beings. This rhythm helps us to maintain a healthy balance of our physical and mental health as it keeps our energy and emotions in check throughout the day.

Being in sync with your ultradian rhythm is essential to manage your time and workload successfully. The ultradian rhythm is a natural cycle of energy and alertness that occurs throughout the day, with one cycle usually lasting between 90 to 120 minutes. You can better manage your work and stress levels by staying in sync with this rhythm.

The key to staying in sync with your ultradian rhythm is to find the right balance between rest and activity, a balance that works for you. You should be aware of when you feel energetic and alert and capitalize on that time to complete your work. Similarly, it would be best to be mindful of when you feel more tired and need rest. By being in sync with your ultradian rhythm, you can ensure that you are working at the proper times, and not overloading yourself with too much work.

Stress is another factor that can interfere with being in sync with your ultradian rhythm. High levels of stress can cause your natural cycle to be disrupted. Taking time to relax and reset your energy levels can help you stay in sync with your ultradian rhythm and manage your workload more effectively.

Avoid Overfilling Your Calendar

One of the most common mistakes people make is overfilling their calendar with too many activities. When you overfill your calendar, there is a good chance that two or perhaps more commitments of yours might clash with each other, putting you in a pickle. Hence it is safe to avoid such situations rather than having to stress yourself out over which commitments you have to attend to first.

The best way to keep your calendar manageable is to prioritize and only commit to important or necessary activities. Consider if the activity will benefit you before agreeing to it. For example, if you're invited to a social gathering, consider whether it's something you'd like to attend and if it's a good use of your time.

It's also helpful to plan ahead and be realistic about how much you can accomplish in a day. Make sure to leave some time slots open for rest in your schedule and for unexpected events or tasks.

Handle the Most Challenging Tasks First

Historically, we have been taught that one of the best ways to get work done faster and quickly is to do the easiest ones first. However, there's an alternate saying that goes, "Handle the most challenging task first, so that you can focus on the easier ones later." And this is a very sound philosophy when it comes to managing your time and reducing stress.

By tackling the most difficult tasks first, you'll be able to focus on the less demanding tasks with greater confidence. This will reduce the time you need to spend on those tasks and free up more energy to deal with more complex matters.

Assign Time to Each Task

Part of the ways you can create your schedule is to ensure that each task has a time limit. Having a schedule reduces procrastination and minimizes wastage of time over unwanted things or places. Working till you are done would be ideal but it is not always practical. Break larger tasks into several sub-tasks, then set a time limit for each. Project management software may help you better organize and manage your tasks and time.

Tame Your Email

Having too many emails can be overwhelming and can cause a lot of stress. It can also lead to time management issues if you don't know how to manage your inbox properly. The best way to manage your emails is to create a system that works for you. Set aside a specific time of day to check your emails and respond to the ones that need to be answered.

A jumbled-up inbox can severely hinder productivity, so creating specific folders for essential emails is a necessity. Additionally, you can set up filters to automatically move emails from certain people or with specific keywords in the subject line into their respective folders. This will help you keep your inbox organized and make it easier to find emails when needed.

Once you have created a system, it is crucial to stick to it. It can be tempting to check your emails throughout the day continuously, but this can lead to unnecessary stress and prevent you from getting other things done.

Instead of spending too much time on your phone or laptop, try to check your emails at the same time each day and limit how much time you spend responding to them. This will help you stay on top of your emails without allowing them to take up too much of your time and overwhelm you.

It is also important to be mindful of the emails you are sending. If you send too many emails, it can be overwhelming for the receiver. Send emails only when necessary and include only the most critical information. This will help reduce stress and reduce the time these emails occupy for all parties involved.

Finally, it is essential to take breaks from your emails. If you get overwhelmed, take a few minutes away from your inbox and do something else.

Delegate and Outsource

Do you often find yourself swamped with too much work but too little time to complete it, whereas your colleague has too little work but the same deadline? Have you wondered if the work assigned to you is beyond your caliber while another team member is assigned work that you have more expertise in? Well, this could be the ill-effects of improper delegating and outsourcing of work by your manager or team leader. Communicate to your manager about your workload and how your time and skills could be better utilized within the company.

If you run your own business and find yourself wearing too many hats with a long list of duties, consider delegating some of those tasks. Delegating and outsourcing can be a great way to manage your time and reduce stress. By delegating tasks and outsourcing them to others, you can free up more time to focus on more important things. This can help you to achieve your goals more quickly and with less stress. When you delegate, provide clear instructions and expectations so your delegate can do their job effectively and efficiently. Also, keeping your workers happy and satisfied is essential if you want your work to be done well.

Always make sure that you reward your delegate for their hard work - this will encourage them to continue working hard.

Practice the Pareto Principle

The Pareto Principle, also known as the 80/20 rule, is a widely accepted principle in business and economics. It states that 80 percent of the effects come from 20 percent of the causes. If you focus your time and energy on the 20 percent of activities that produce the most results, you can get more done in less time and put yourself through less stress.

Time management is an integral part of the Pareto Principle. By focusing on the 20 percent of activities that will yield the most significant results, you can dramatically reduce the amount of time you spend on activities that don't bring you closer to your goals. This can mean anything from focusing on the tasks that will make the most significant impact on your goals to delegating tasks that can be done by someone else. This can free up much of your time and allow you to focus on the most critical tasks. Focusing on the most important 20 percent of activities makes you less likely to be overwhelmed.

Take Advantage of the Employee Assistance Program

Last but not least, if you are dealing with an overwhelming issue that is outside the scope of your workload but is still affecting the quality of your work, such as dealing with grief, abuse, or other personal matters, it would be wise to take advantage of any employee assistance program that is available at your place of employment or to seek professional help. Allowing personal issues to fester and seep into your workplace will eventually compound your workplace stress. Additionally, letting your coworkers know you're dealing with some personal matters without going into too much detail can help others exercise greater patience and tolerance with you.

Examine Your Workplace Boundaries

Have you ever given thought to your personal boundaries at work? If not, here are some great questions to start with:

- Do you often willingly take on your coworkers' work?

- Do you find it hard to communicate with your manager or refuse when you're being handed too much work?

- When was the last time you spent some quality time with your loved ones? And how often do you do that?

- When was the last time you came into work feeling refreshed and energized to work?

What were your answers? Did you realize whether something was amiss? Was it all as it should be?

We have made some great progress and are on to the final stretch. In our final chapter, we will address the cares and needs of the most important and well-deserved person, YOU! We will discuss proven strategies and techniques that will help you relieve the pressures and find lasting relief - let's do this!

Chapter 6

From Burnout to Bliss

"How you love yourself is how you teach others to love you."
~ Rupi Kaur

Kami was a successful entrepreneur, and her business was flourishing. However, she had been pushing herself too hard for far too long, and it had started to take a toll on her physical and mental health. Despite being aware of the importance of self-care, she had never truly prioritized it. However, everything changed when she faced a major health scare.

Ignoring her symptoms and persevering through work, Kami eventually collapsed and was rushed to the hospital. She was diagnosed with a serious health condition that required immediate treatment.

The doctors told Kami that her condition was a result of her high-stress lifestyle and neglecting her self-care. Kami was devastated. She had always believed that working hard was paramount, only to realize that it had nearly cost her her life.

After her health scare, Kami was forced to take time off work to focus on her recovery. She decided to utilize this time in making drastic changes to her lifestyle. She started to exercise regularly, eat healthy, and get enough sleep. She also started to prioritize activities that made her feel happy and fulfilled.

Initially, prioritizing self-care proved challenging for Kami, given her deeply ingrained belief that success relied solely on hard work. However, as she continued to practice self-care, she began to see positive changes in her life. She felt happier, healthier, and more energized.

Upon returning to work, Kami embraced a transformed perspective on life. She realized that taking care of herself was essential for a happy and fulfilling life rather than just working hard at the expense of everything else.

Experiences like Kami's can be a real eye-opener for many, but you don't have to reach that point to realize how critical self-care is for your physical and mental health.

Self-care is an essential part of life that can help us manage stress, prevent burnout, and keep us healthy. It can be easy to forget to take care of ourselves, but it is one of the most important things we can do for our physical and mental well-being. Self-care encompasses various activities, from basic everyday tasks like eating nutritious meals and getting enough sleep to more intentional practices such as meditation, journaling, and scheduling leisure activities. This improves our capacity to live fully, vibrantly, and productively.

Self-care also serves as a reminder to you and others that your needs are a priority and should be treated as such. Self-care strengthens your relationship with the essence of who you are so that you can stay anchored and prevent yourself from getting carried away even when times get tough. It keeps you from getting overwhelmed and helps you to stop worrying about trivial things. Developing the habit of self-care will help you understand who you are, identify your passions and purposes, and put you on the road to living a happy and content life.

Practicing Self-Care

Katie Reed made this profound statement, "*Self-care is giving the world the best of you, instead of what's left of you.*"

Self-care can look different to different people. It's essential to take the time to identify the things that make you feel relaxed, energized, and fulfilled. This could include reading a book, going for a walk, listening to music, spending time with friends, or even getting a massage. It is essential to recognize what works for you and to utilize it as a form of self-care effectively.

Many people find it challenging to prioritize self-care. While some may believe that practicing self-care is selfish, nothing could be further from the truth. Taking care of oneself is essential to giving you the stamina to be able to care for others. So, it is essential to love yourself first to be able to love anybody else without any regrets. It's not called being selfish, it's called self-love.

Benefits of Practicing Self-Care

While self-care can often seem like a luxury, it is, in fact, an essential part of leading a healthy, productive life. There are numerous benefits to self-care, including improved physical and mental health, improved relationships, increased self-confidence and self-esteem, better stress management, greater resilience in difficult situations, and improved decision-making ability.

By practicing self-care, you are creating a different version of yourself, a better and healthier version, thus paving the way for a better tomorrow not just for yourself but for those around you as well. Let us see what the various benefits of practicing self-care are.

Self-Care Can Aid With Stress Management

Small, manageable quantities of stress might help you stay motivated to complete a task, but sustained stress and worry can be harmful to both your physical and mental health. Engaging in self-care practices such as meditation or seeking support from loved ones can help alleviate the negative impact of stress. These activities can uplift your mood, boost energy levels, and enhance self-confidence.

Your Relationship With Your Partner Improves

Self-care is a vital component of any successful relationship, and it's essential to recognize its impact on your relationship with your partner. Taking care of your own needs and feelings helps create a strong foundation of trust and mutual respect, both of which are essential to a successful relationship. Nurturing yourself contributes to maintaining a positive connection with your partner.

One of the most important aspects of self-care is cultivating self-respect, as it helps to ensure you are honoring your needs and feelings. By prioritizing your emotional well-being, you become better equipped to navigate challenges within the relationship, which helps avoid letting any challenge negatively affect your relationship.

Another way that self-care can improve your relationship with your partner is by helping you to understand your own needs and feelings better. When you take the time to focus on yourself, it can help increase your awareness about your own thoughts and emotions. This can help you communicate more effectively with your partner about what you need and expect from the relationship.

Furthermore, self-care can also help you to be better equipped to handle difficult emotions. When you're struggling with anxiety or burnout, it can be hard to focus on your partner's needs. Taking the time to practice self-care can help you manage your emotions better to be more present and emotionally available for your partner and help them deal with their tough times as well. Taking the time to practice self-care can go a long way in improving your relationship with your partner.

Self-Care Habits to Practice

Self-care is not just about taking time for yourself and getting a massage. Self-care is essential to building your resilience, maintaining your mental and physical health, and creating a life you love. Taking care of yourself doesn't mean wallowing in self-pity or being selfish. It means recognizing your true potential, recognizing just how much you have to offer the world, so much to contribute from within, and so many things to look forward to. It also doesn't mean putting off everything until later. Self-care means making small changes in the present that will help you adjust better in the future. Even if you haven't thought much about self-care previously, there are plenty of things you can start doing right away to improve your well-being on the inside as well as on the outside. Here are some self-care habits to practice:

Make Use of Meditation

The term meditation originated from the Latin word "meditatum," which means "to ponder/measure." A study showed that more than 14 percent of people in the US have tried meditating at least once.

Meditation has been used for centuries to help individuals deal with stress. It is an effective and natural way to reduce and manage stress and prevent burnout. Meditation has been scientifically proven to reduce the physical and psychological effects of stress and can be used to improve mental and physical well-being.

There are various ways in which meditation can be utilized to reduce stress. You can induce relaxation in both your body and mind, fostering the ability to observe thoughts, feelings, and sensations without judgment or attachment. This results in inner peace and clarity.

Meditation can help you to reduce the physical effects of stress, such as increased heart rate and muscle tension, as well as the psychological impacts of stress, such as excessive worrying and rumination. It supports the development of a balanced perspective, enabling focus on the present moment, gratitude for what one has, and acknowledgment of personal limitations.

Hydrotherapy

Bathing is one of the simplest self-care rituals you can do. It's not only refreshing but it can also help relieve stress and improve your mood by releasing endorphins, hormones that affect your mood and cause pleasure. The Romans valued hydrotherapy as a fancy way of expressing that water has therapeutic properties. Here are a couple of reasons why bathing is a crucial component of self-care:

1) Bathing helps you to relax your mind and body. When you bathe, you get wet and cool off - two things known to help reduce stress and increase relaxation.

2) Bathing helps to refresh your spirit and make you feel more positive and energetic.

Embrace Nature

Grounding is a self-care practice that helps to relieve stress and improve overall well-being. It is a process of connecting with the Earth through your senses. In doing so, you are also connecting with your body and mind to calm and center yourself. When you ground yourself, you're telling your body that you're safe and comfortable.

There are a few ways to ground yourself. You can spend time in nature, walk barefoot outdoors, or do simple outdoor activities like gardening or smelling fresh flowers. Spending time outside is a healthy activity for self-care. Your blood flow is improved, inflammation is reduced, and you get a better night's sleep when you regularly keep your feet on the ground.

You can also ground yourself with music or artwork. Grounding can be done in several ways. Just like every other form of self-care, you need to experiment a little and find out what works best for you. The key is to remain consistent. Grounding is a valuable tool that empowers you to regain control of your well-being and enhance overall happiness.

Deep Breathing

Deep breathing is one of the most powerful and effective tools for self-care and relieving stress. Focusing on your breathing can reduce your stress and anxiety levels and re-energize your body and mind. Deep breathing can be done anywhere, anytime, and it is an easy way to take time out for yourself and focus on your well-being. In fact, deep breathing doesn't improve just your mental health but your physical health as well. It boosts your metabolism and suppresses your appetite, thus helping in regulating your weight as well.

When we feel stressed, our breath tends to become shallow and rapid. Taking a few deep breaths can help to slow down your heart rate and relax your body. We can activate the body's relaxation response by taking slow, deep breaths. Deep breathing also helps to increase oxygenation in the body, which can help to boost energy levels. It also increases endorphins, the body's natural stress-relieving hormones.

Deep breathing can be done in any setting and can be done for as little as a few minutes a day. To practice deep breathing:

1. Find a comfortable, quiet spot where you won't be disturbed.

2. Close your eyes and focus on your breath.

3. Start by taking slow, deep breaths in and out, inhaling through your nose and exhaling through your mouth.

4. Focus on your breath and how it feels in your body as you breathe.

5. Pay attention to the sensation of your breath as it enters and leaves your body.

Continue this practice for several minutes, focusing on each breath and allowing yourself to relax. With each breath, feel the tension in your body slowly releasing. At the end of your deep breathing session, take some time to notice how your body and mind feel and any other changes you may have noticed.

Deep breathing can also be combined with visualization techniques to help you relax and reduce stress. Visualize a calming and peaceful environment, such as a beach or a forest. Imagine the sound of waves crashing on the shore or birds singing in the trees. Immerse yourself in the soothing atmosphere and fully embrace the sense of calm and peace.

At times when you feel stressed out or anxious, deep breathing can help you regain control. It is a simple self-care practice that can help you relieve stress and improve your overall well-being. Take the time to practice deep breathing and make it a part of your daily self-care routine. With consistent effort, you will develop the ability to use deep breathing to effectively manage stress and maintain emotional equilibrium.

Exercise

Finding time to work out every day might be challenging for those with busy schedules. However, if you spend the majority of your day in front of a computer, you need to find ways to include exercise in your schedule. Simple steps like walking your dog, taking the stairs, or parking further away are sufficient. An excellent way to add exercise to your day is to clean your house or do a dance workout. Additionally, many fitness programs today—or even fitness YouTube videos—offer quick workouts that may be completed in as little as 10 minutes. You are more likely to stick to a workout if it is enjoyable.

Build Self-Confidence

"The way to develop self-confidence is to do the thing you fear and get a record of successful experiences behind you" is a piece of well heed advice by William Jennings Bryan.

There's no one-size-fits-all solution to building self-confidence, but you can do a few things to help. First, be patient. Developing self-confidence takes time and effort. The more you work on it, the better you'll feel. The new version of yourself that you end up with will be worth all the patience and practice you put into building your self-confidence.

Second, remember that self-confidence is a cumulative process - it won't happen overnight. It takes time and experience to develop a strong sense of self-worth, and it won't happen if you don't keep working at it. You can't expect to observe changes in yourself within a few days or weeks. Building your confidence is a slow and prolonged process but it is well worth the effort.

Finally, keep in mind that self-confidence is something that you can improve, even if you don't have all the answers. There are plenty of resources out there that can help you build your self-confidence, and the more you use them, the better you'll feel.

Here are some tips to help you take the necessary steps to build your self-confidence.

First, set small goals for yourself. Setting realistic goals and working towards them can be a great way to boost self-confidence. Start with something small and achievable, then move on to bigger goals. Once you have achieved a goal, take the time to celebrate and recognize your hard work. Appreciating your efforts is a great way to increase your self-esteem.

Secondly, practice positive thinking. Focusing on the positive and being kind to yourself is integral to building self-confidence. Avoid making negative statements about yourself. Instead, focus on the positive aspects of yourself. If you start to have negative thoughts, take a few deep breaths and remind yourself that you are capable and worthy.

Thirdly, surround yourself with positive people. The people you choose to spend time with can significantly impact your confidence. Spend time with supportive people who believe in you and will help to encourage and motivate you when necessary.

Take Naps

There's no doubt that napping is a great way to improve your overall health and well-being. Not only is napping a great way to recharge and re-energize your body and mind, but it can also help to improve your mood, concentration, and energy levels. And the best part is that napping is easy - you can do it anywhere, any time.

Do you usually reach for a cup of coffee when you get into that afternoon slump? If you do, it may be just as beneficial and even healthier to take a 20-minute siesta or nap instead. In a study conducted by NASA on military pilots and astronauts, it found that a 40-minute nap improved their performance by 34 percent, and alertness by a whopping 100 percent. Well, you don't have to necessarily take such long naps, but this goes to show that even a short nap of 15-20 minutes can greatly improve alertness, concentration, and performance.

Napping can also help you recover from the effects of sleep deprivation, such as fatigue and irritability, which are very common in those who experience burnout. It can also help you to be more productive and energized by improving your concentration, memory, and alertness.

Another benefit of taking naps is improved cognitive functioning. Studies have shown that regular naps can help to enhance problem-solving skills and creativity. Finally, napping can help to improve our physical health. Research has shown that frequent naps can help to lower our risk of heart disease and stroke. It can also help improve our immune system by reducing inflammation.

Limit Social Media

Social media is like a coin with both pros and cons. On one side of the coin are the pros, such as the fact that social media keeps us connected, provides us with entertainment, and that it is undeniably one of the best platforms to showcase our talents. On the other side, though, an addiction to social media can cause you undue stress, anxiety, and depression, make you vulnerable to identity theft and many other cyber-crimes, and the list goes on.

According to a 2020 survey conducted by DataReportal, it was found that the average person spent nearly 2 hours and 24 minutes a day using social media in 2020, which was equal to more than a month of their year.

Social media can be a great way to connect with friends and family, but it can also be a source of stress and anxiety. It's important to remember that social media is a tool, not a destination. If you're using social media to avoid dealing with your problems, you're likely to end up feeling worse than before. Instead, use social media how it's meant to be used. Use it to connect with friends and family and do not forgo taking care of yourself in the process. By limiting how much time you spend on social media, you can ensure that you are engaging in healthy social media habits and not letting it take over your life. Here are some ways to put a time limit on your social media:

The first is to set a timer. Decide how much time you want to spend on social media each day. Set up a timer, and once it goes off, make sure you log off and take a break. This will help you stay on target and make sure you don't get too absorbed in social media.

The second way is to delete social media apps from your phone or tablet. This will make it harder to access social media, and you'll be more likely to find something else to do. This can greatly help you stay focused and productive.

A third way to limit time spent on social media is to turn off notifications. This will help you stay focused on the task and not get distracted by notifications from social media sites. You can also use a website blocker to prevent yourself from accessing certain websites.

Finally, if you check social media too often, try to find a hobby or activity to help you stay off social media. This could be anything from reading a book to taking a walk outside surrounded by nature or spending time with friends or family members. Remember, take your eyes off the screen and take your time enjoying the green.

Walk During Lunchtime

Did you know walking can make you smarter? Yes, you read that right. In 2011, a study conducted by the University of Illinois showed that walking for 40 minutes three times a week increases the size of the hippocampus, the part of the brain responsible for storing memory and learning.

Take a thoughtful stroll every day at noon or during break time to benefit your physical health and take a break to try and relieve any stress you may be experiencing at work. Depending on how long your lunch break is, consider taking a 20 to 30-minute stroll in an area near your workplace after eating.

It will give you a much-needed breath of fresh air and enable you to detach from your job and any stress associated with it. It'll improve your mood significantly and when you return to your desk, you will have a renewed sense of vigor and your productivity at work will also take a hike. Bring a coworker with you if you want someone to talk with during your stroll. Furthermore, making time to walk more and move around has many health benefits, especially if you have a sedentary job.

Play Music While Working

Playing music while working is one strategy for reducing work-related stress. Even though not everyone may find it useful, for some, listening to their favorite tunes can make the workday go by faster, increase productivity, and help them relax. Music can be a good distraction from external noise, and it can also inspire creativity and innovation.

Practicing Mindfulness

Mindfulness has become increasingly popular in recent years and for good reason. Practicing mindfulness can help you relieve stress, improve self-care, and overall foster a stronger connection to your emotions. When you practice mindfulness, you train your brain to be more aware and responsive, enabling you to recognize unhelpful reactions and take a step back to observe your experiences instead of letting them affect you negatively. Through consistent practice, you can develop a heightened awareness of how your thoughts, emotions, and physical sensations interact, empowering you to respond in a more mindful manner.

It is important to remember that mindfulness is a skill that requires regular practice in order to fully reap its benefits. So, make sure to set aside some time each day to practice mindfulness. The amount of time you want to dedicate each day depends entirely on you and your needs. You can dedicate as little as five minutes or as long as you need. Keep in mind that perfection is not the goal, nor is getting it right on the first attempt. Practice makes perfect, so be kind to yourself as you practice persistently.

Exercise Mindfulness at Work

Mindfulness is an excellent practice for self-care and relieving stress in the workplace. It can enhance focus, productivity, and facilitate a deeper connection with yourself and your surroundings. Here are a few ways to incorporate mindfulness at work:

Take a few moments throughout the day to pause and take a few deep breaths. This can help you to reset by clearing your mind, which will help you rejuvenate and heighten your awareness of your environment.

Additionally, practicing mindfulness by listening without judgment or expectation can foster more meaningful conversations.

Be mindful of your emotions throughout the day. Check in with yourself from time to time to assess your feelings and consider whether your emotional state is where you want it to be or not. This can help you stay in tune with your body and emotions.

Finally, make sure to take regular breaks throughout the day. Set a timer to remind yourself and get up from your desk and move around. A few minutes of physical activity, be it stretching, walking, or standing, can clear your mind and provide a much-needed break to both your mind and body.

If you're finding it difficult to stay mindful at work, try incorporating mindfulness into your routine. Make it a priority to practice mindfulness, whether that means setting reminders for yourself or taking a few moments throughout the day to pause and be present.

Practice Self-Compassion

Self-compassion is a powerful tool that can help you to manage your stress levels. It can be defined as treating oneself with kindness and understanding when things don't go as planned or when we feel overwhelmed. There will always be multiple points in life where we fail, stumble, or fall short of our desired outcome. In vulnerable moments like these, it is crucial to be kind and understanding towards ourselves. It's important to recognize when we feel distressed and to remind ourselves that it's not necessary to be resilient through every difficulty.

Self-compassion enables us to release negative thoughts and emotions, replacing them with positive and realistic ones. It also allows you to recognize and accept your struggles and challenges. Rather than expecting ourselves to "suck it up" and move on, we must show kindness and understanding when our expectations are not met. It's essential to recognize our suffering and accept that life is full of challenging moments and that sometimes, we ourselves are the cause of them. Self-compassion means recognizing our shared humanity and extending ourselves a bit of compassion and grace just like we would to someone else in our position.

Practicing self-compassion greatly improves your ability to cope with difficult emotions and situations, leading to increased understanding and compassion for oneself and others. It also enhances resilience when facing tough times.

Many people often overlook the notion of being kind to oneself, thinking that it will simply encourage a habit of making excuses for bad conduct or taking part in excessive pleasures. However, research shows several advantages to exercising self-compassion. Those who show compassion for themselves are more likely to:

1. Pick themself off the ground after failing and try again.

2. Hold themself accountable for their actions, especially when they are at fault.

3. They are more resilient to negative feedback because they know they have intrinsic worth and aptitude.

How to Build Self-Compassion

Journal It

Write about it and journal your thoughts and feelings. Putting your thoughts and feelings on paper is valuable, even if you believe you're not skilled at it. When put on paper, your thoughts are more than just weightless sentences swirling in your head; they gain substance, form, and life. They become real, reinforcing your belief in them. It helps reassure you that your feelings are valid.

Confide in a Friend

If you're not much of a writer, talking about your feelings helps, too. It validates your thoughts and heals you from within. Choose carefully whom you confide in, as toxic individuals may exploit your vulnerabilities and manipulate your emotions. Talking to a good friend or even a therapist is a good idea in such times. Ask your friends for help, brainstorm your troubles, and you'll feel like a huge weight has just been lifted off your chest.

Know Yourself Well

Observe yourself more closely the same way you would someone else. How does your mind observe others when they talk negatively to you or try to talk you down? Consider all your feelings, positive as well as negative. Allow your feelings to flow naturally and stop fighting the content that comes with it. Embrace acceptance, as it paves the way for a healthy relationship with your mind.

Indulge in Quiet Time

Allow for some quiet time. Enjoy a cup of coffee on your balcony or savor tea in peaceful solitude. Your soul craves stillness away from the humdrum of bustling life. Spend time in nature and walk barefoot on the grass. Grant your senses a much-needed break from the constant influx of information.

Limit Toxic Relationships

Toxic relationships can be a significant source of stress and anxiety. It is vital to limit the influence of these relationships to ensure our own mental and emotional well-being. Recognizing toxic relationships can be challenging when we are in them.

There are certain signs to watch out for, such as frequent arguments, feeling drained after interactions, lack of respect, and a sense of inappreciation for your efforts in the relationship. If you feel drained, anxious, or frustrated after spending time with someone, it is an indication that the relationship may be detrimental to your mental health. It is also important to note that toxic relationships are not just limited to romantic relationships. Friendships, family relationships, and work relationships can all be toxic.

Once we identify a toxic relationship, limiting our exposure to it is important. We can do this by setting boundaries, such as limiting how often we interact with the person, only talking to them in certain environments, or even avoiding them altogether. Prioritizing self-care and building a supportive network of individuals who make us feel safe and valued is extremely important.

It is important to remember that we cannot change other people, but we can change how we respond to them and how much contact we have with them, thereby limiting how their negative behavior affects us. Limiting exposure to toxic relationships can effectively reduce stress and create a healthier environment for personal growth. Limiting toxic relationships can be difficult, but it is critical for our well-being.

Positive Affirmations

Our words possess incredible power. They can weaken the strongest person and strengthen the weakest person. Because of this, we must be mindful of how we use our words on others as well as on ourselves. One beneficial approach to employ during times of burnout is the practice of positive affirmations.

Positive affirmations are a powerful tool to help us shape our perception of ourselves and our lives. These simple yet impactful statements assist in reprogramming our subconscious mind and foster positive transformations. Positive affirmations are a way to reprogram our brains to think differently and focus on what we want instead of what we don't want.

When we use positive affirmations, we actively create a positive mindset and reinforce positive self-talk. This practice enables us to break old habits, establish new ones, and replace limiting beliefs with empowering ones. They can also allow us to increase our self-confidence and self-belief, focus on our goals, and manifest our desires.

Positive affirmations can be utilized in many different ways, such as writing them down, reading them aloud, using visualization, or listening to them. They are a powerful way to shift our mindset and create positive changes in our life. They can help us to focus on our goals and manifest our desires.

Consistency and intentionality are key to ensuring you utilize positive affirmations effectively. Make sure to repeat them often, and use positive, empowering language when you do. When engaging in positive affirmations, it is important to evoke the accompanying emotions and genuinely believe in the words we express. When we do this, our subconscious mind will start to believe what we are saying and begin to create positive changes in our life.

Concept of Self-Affirmation

The self-affirmation theory was first made public by Claude Steele, a social psychologist and professor at Stanford University, in the late 1980s. The approach focuses on how people adjust to knowledge or events that threaten their sense of self. According to the self-affirmation idea, if you concentrate on the values you wish to uphold, you'll be less likely to feel stressed out and respond defensively when faced with an experience or piece of information that challenges or threatens your sense of self.

Self-Affirmations and Scientific Research

The creation of the self-affirmation idea has sparked neuroscientific research that aims to determine whether positive self-affirmation actually causes any changes in the brain.

Neuroplasticity is a scientific concept that explains how we can modify our brains with the words we use. While younger individuals have an easier time adapting to new thought processes, as we age, our thinking becomes more rigid. Neuro-Linguistic Programming explores the notion that our language can effectively program our minds and that the results of our thoughts can be seen in the real world.

A study conducted by psychologists from Stanford University and the University of California revealed that affirmations had the power to prevent the spiral of negativity. As part of the same research, positive affirmations improved relationships and health outcomes, all the while positively influencing our brain's reward systems.

The self-affirmation theory should not be confused with the New Age concept of self-affirmation. While there are similarities between the two approaches, it is important to note that they are not the same. In contrast, the New Age concept of self-affirmation often involves more spiritual or metaphysical practices and is not based on scientific evidence. This includes spiritual meditation, yoga, and visualization exercises. These practices focus more on cultivating a sense of inner peace and connection with a higher power. They are less concerned with reinforcing positive beliefs about oneself and more centered on fostering a deeper sense of inner tranquility and connection with a higher power.

The Three P's of Affirmations

1. **Positive.** Structure your affirmations in a positive statement. Avoid using don't, not, won't, or can't in your affirmations, as these are associated with negative thoughts. For example, instead of saying, "I don't want to fail this exam," say instead, "I am doing well on this exam."

2. **Present.** Use the present tense, conveying that the affirmation is happening in the current moment. Steer clear of future phrases tense such as "I am going" or "I will." For example, instead of

saying, "I am going to lose weight," say instead, "It feels good to be losing weight."

3. **Personal.** Personalize your affirmation instead of having it dependent on outside factors, which are often out of your control. For example, instead of saying, "My mate will be happy with my new hairstyle," say instead, "I am happy with my new hairstyle." As a side note, try incorporating the word "I" without using the interrogative adverb "when."

Examples of Self-Affirmations

To *Improve Your Mood*

While positive affirmations are not exactly a treatment for depression by themselves, they can be quite effective if used appropriately. According to a study conducted at the University of Arizona, affirmations can be helpful as a supplemental treatment for many depressed or anxious individuals. Optimistic thinking has the ability to challenge depressive thoughts, and repeating positive affirmations can help reshape thought processes.

The following are some of the most effective ones for treating depression:

I am powerful.

I adore who I am.

I have complete affection for myself.

To maximize the benefits, it is recommended to vocalize these affirmations each time a negative thought arises.

To *Help Your Stay Motivated*

As you begin your day, select one of the affirmations below and write it on a Post-it note. (You can also download these for free on our website: www.thepagepress.com/resources) Place the note where you can see it throughout the day, like on the side of your computer screen, in your planner, or on a wall. Take a moment several times throughout your day to pause and reflect on the written note audibly or in your head. This practice will help you establish a positive mindset for the day, regardless of how it unfolds.

I have the power to change my story.

I am grateful for everything I have in my life.

I am okay.

I am calm.

I forgive myself.

I am healing each day.

Today is a great day.

I have the courage to say no.

I am good enough.

I belong here.

I accept who I am now and can change into whatever I want to be.

I am led by my dreams.

I have value and worth.

Today will be a productive day.

I am strong.

I choose hope over fear.

I choose to be positive.

I believe in myself.

I am getting healthier every day.

I am closer to achieving my goals.

I am a better person today.

My actions are meaningful and inspiring.

I have a good heart.

Happiness is a choice, and I choose to be happy.

I am at peace with myself.

Relaxation Techniques

While it is not always easy to avoid stress, there are ways to cope, such as practicing relaxation techniques. Relaxation techniques are often simple to learn and can be employed in any situation to cultivate a sense of calm and tranquility. They can help clear the mind, reduce physical tension, and promote a positive attitude overall. Whether you're looking for a quick stress-relief solution or a more comprehensive approach to relaxation, there are many techniques available to help you find the right solution according to your needs. Relaxation techniques provide an easy way to take a break from the hustle and bustle of our daily lives and focus on ourselves. By dedicating time each day to practice these techniques, stress levels can be reduced, leading to a healthier and more fulfilling life. Below are several relaxation techniques; find one that works best for you.

Deep Breathing Technique

Deep breathing is a relaxation technique that involves focusing on your breath, inhaling deeply for relaxation, and exhaling to release stress. If you're having trouble with taking big breaths, remind yourself that you're picking up a new respiration technique. It may take a bit of exercise before you can master it. Commit to practicing several times a week, or ideally daily, as the frequency of practice will make it easier over time.

1. Taking deep breaths into your stomach is essential for reducing stress. When you are anxious, you may tend to take short breaths into your upper chest. As you inhale, your diaphragm should move downward, causing your abdomen to expand. Make sure to allow the air to reach the bottom of your abdomen. (If you find it hard to breathe while sitting, you can stand in a comfortable stance with your feet about shoulder-width apart, knees straight but not locked, and arms hanging freely with shoulders relaxed.)

2. Expel all of the air from your lungs via your mouth. You'll feel your stomach muscles tightening as you release all the breath from your body.

3. Draw in a steady breath through your nostrils and observe your belly expand. Visualize the air entering your body, supplying it with new, invigorating oxygen, beginning at the lower abdomen and gradually reaching the higher areas of your lungs.

4. Take a deep breath in, and then let every last bit of air out. Slowing down your breathing will bring about a sense of relaxation. Take at least three long, deep breaths to bring some quick relief and 10 minutes to reach a deeper state of relaxation.

Autogenic Relaxation

Suggestive relaxation is a technique that utilizes explicit verbal recommendations to induce physical relaxation, much like meditation. Here is a step-by-step guide to practicing autogenic relaxation:

1. Repeat the phrase, "My left hand is heavy. My left hand is heavy. I am tranquil, and my left hand is heavy" to yourself repeatedly for

one minute. If any distracting thoughts come up, just let them go and keep repeating the same phrase.

2. Verbally declare the following: "My left hand feels heavy. My right hand is also heavy. I feel tranquil, and my right hand is still heavy." Continue saying this for the next 60 seconds.

3. Utter the words over and over again for each body part, such as foot, arm, leg, and eventually the entire body in the line. If you want, you can repeat the whole pattern a second time. Make a habit of practicing this technique regularly (multiple times a week or even every day) and remember that practice makes perfect!

Progressive Muscle Relaxation

Progressive muscle relaxation is a technique that focuses on specific areas of the physique. By tensing and then releasing the muscles, you can differentiate between tension and relaxation. If you find any discomfort with this approach, feel free to try an alternative method. Here is a step-by-step guide to practicing progressive muscle relaxation:

1. Start by curling your hands into tight fists as you take note of the sensation of tightness surrounding your skin. Remain in this position and observe the uneasiness that comes with attempting to maintain your fists in this position. Once the tension becomes unbearable, loosen your grip and take note of the feeling of relief that spreads through your hand (i.e., the sensation of heat that washes over your hand).

2. Bend your feet, pulling the front of them up towards your knees while the toes are clenched. When it becomes uncomfortable, let your feet relax and observe the sensation of heat as the muscles loosen.

3. Progress to other areas of the body such as your arms, legs, abdominal area and torso, and eventually your neck and head.

Guided Imagery Relaxation

Guided imagery is a form of relaxation that requires creating a vivid mental image (e.g., a stroll along the shoreline). This practice, analogous to a managed fantasy, assists the mind in blocking out stressful ideas and diminishing physical tension. Here is a step-by-step guide to practicing guided imagery:

1. Begin by taking a deep breath, inhaling through your nostrils, and exhaling through your mouth.

2. Visualize something that is appealing and calming to you. Imagery could range from a stroll in the woods or on the shoreline to recollecting your most beloved areas or occurrences. The most significant part of exercising guided imagery is having enough detail to take yourself to a state of tranquility.

3. When you are concluding your session, travel mentally back to the starting point of the visualization and then slowly count from 10 down to 1 before opening your eyes.

Getting On Your (Vagus) Nerve

"You're getting on my nerves!" I'm sure we've all said it ourselves or, at least, heard it being said at some point (hopefully, not about us). I don't know how that idiom came to be, but there is some truth to it. We're talking about the vagus nerve, to be specific. Never heard of it? Neither had I until I was invited to a webinar about it. What is it, and why should you care?

Your vagus nerve contains thousands of fibers that extend from your brain stem and travels to your heart, lungs, kidneys, digestive tract, and spleen. It serves as a two-way communication highway relaying information from your internal organs to your brain. Data is also sent out from your brain to control your organ functions, like heart rate, breathing, and reflexes. The vagus nerve plays a significant role in your parasympathetic nervous system, better known as your flight or fight response.

When your body remains in a prolonged state of stress, it becomes crucial to stimulate your vagus nerve to promote rejuvenation and recovery of both mind and body. Doing exercises to stimulate the vagus nerve at home can enhance your vagal tone, which is the capacity of the vagus nerve to control your heart rate. This allows your body to revert to a calm state quicker after a tense experience. It is crucial to ensure that situations that stress out your mind and body are short-lived and that you enter into a state of recovery shortly after. This is beneficial in achieving peak concentration, great performance, and all of the other elements we are concerned about. It signifies that your body possesses the flexibility to find balance despite being exposed to demanding inner or outer stimuli.

Vagus nerve exercises aim to redirect your attention to the body instead of the racing mind. When we lose control of our problem-solving brains, they fixate on what we cannot control. But wisdom traditions, which count on this as the root of much suffering, agree that training the vagus nerve to focus on what we can control is quite powerful. Regularly practicing vagus nerve exercises can lead to a rapid decrease in the influence of the sympathetic nervous system, which is associated with the "fight or flight" response, within minutes.

Exercise #1: Breathing

When you regulate your breathing, you disrupt feedback loops that might otherwise intensify stress. During inhalation, the heart rate speeds up. During exhalation, the vagus nerve slows the frequency of heartbeats via actions on the parasympathetic nervous system. When you breathe out slowly, you feel calmer.

Here's how to practice the technique:

1. Find a comfortable seated position with your back supported.

Place your tongue against the upper front teeth and maintain this position throughout the exercise.

2. Begin by making a "woosh" sound as you exhale completely, then inhale quietly for four seconds through your nose. Breathe from the diaphragm rather than the chest for four seconds.

3. Hold your breath for seven seconds, then exhale audibly through rounded lips for eight seconds. This is one round.

There are four rounds in a set. The key to the exercise is to extend your exhalations for twice as long as your inhalations, which should be reached after four sets.

Exercise #2: Singing, Humming, or Listening to Music

The vagus nerve controls the muscles in the larynx (voice box) that allow you to produce sound. When you engage in activities like singing or humming, you exhale for longer periods than you inhale. This prolonged exhale creates vibrations that stimulate the muscles in the throat, which in turn communicate with the vagus nerve.

Another way to stimulate the vagus nerve is by listening to music. The best music to induce relaxation should have a slow tempo, no lyrics, and a simple melody. Think spa music. The optimal listening time to experience the effects is around 13 minutes.

In a study done by Music as Medicine, they reported that out of its 7,581 participants, 79% reported a reduction in muscle tension, 84% experienced a decrease in negative thoughts, 91% felt a greater sense of contentment, and 82% reported improved sleep after engaging with music.

By singing, humming, or listening to relaxing music, you can activate the vagus nerve and enjoy the associated benefits of reduced muscle tension, reduced negative thoughts, increased contentment, and improved sleep.

Exercise #3: Touching

Vagus fibers present in the skin are connected to pressure sensors, allowing for the perception of touch and leading to vagus nerve stimulation. This stimulation affects the hypothalamic and neuroendocrine systems, which regulate the nervous system and the release of stress hormones such as cortisol.

When you give or receive a massage, the same pressure receptors in your fingers are activated as when someone gives you a hug or pet. Similarly, the act of hugging, receiving or giving a massage, or stroking a beloved pet activates these pressure receptors.

Remember that just like any other exercise, consistency is key when you are practicing these exercises. Regular or daily practice will ensure quicker and more effective results. Over time, the same amount of time and effort will result in a greater impact.

Laughter Therapy

It has been figuratively stated that laughter is the best medicine, but there is definitely some truth to this saying. In the medical field, laughter therapy is a form of psychotherapy that uses humor and laughter to encourage mental and physical healing. It is based on the idea that laughter is a powerful form of self-expression that can help people cope with their problems and reduce stress. Laughter therapy aims to improve overall health and well-being by helping people relax, reduce stress, increase positive emotions, and create a sense of connection with others.

Laughter therapy can be particularly effective in managing difficult emotions such as anger, sadness, and anxiety. It also assists individuals in managing their stress levels, which helps manage other negative emotions as well and cultivating a greater sense of joy and optimism in life.

Laughter therapy is typically conducted in groups and can involve activities such as telling jokes, watching funny movies and clips, and playing laughter games. Its effectiveness is enhanced when practiced in a secure and supportive environment.

Physical Benefits of Laughter

In addition to helping people to feel calmer and more connected, laughter therapy can also help to improve physical health. Research has indicated that laughter can enhance the immune system, reduce levels of the stress hormone cortisol, and even alleviate physical pain.

Relaxes Muscle

When you're anxious, your body tends to tense up. However, engaging in a hearty laugh can provide physical relief and help relax your muscles for up to 45 minutes.

Enhances Cardiovascular Health

Research has demonstrated that laughter can have a positive impact on our heart health and cardiovascular system in several ways.

Firstly, laughter helps to reduce stress by triggering the release of endorphins, which are hormones that promote relaxation. This can help to lower blood pressure, reduce the risk of heart attack and stroke, and even improve overall circulation. Furthermore, laughter has been shown to have anti-inflammatory effects, which can contribute to a lower risk of cardiovascular disease.

Secondly, laughter increases the oxygenation of the blood. When we laugh, our diaphragm and lungs expand, allowing more oxygen to enter our bloodstream. This increased oxygen supply lowers the risk of heart attack and stroke and improves overall cardiovascular health.

Thirdly, laughter increases heart rate, which helps to improve circulation and blood flow. This can help reduce the risk of heart attack and stroke and improve overall cardiovascular health.

Finally, laughter can help reduce the risk of atherosclerosis, which is plaque buildup in the arteries. Studies have found that laughter can help to reduce the amount of plaque in the arteries, which can help to reduce the risk of heart attack and stroke.

Boosts Immune System

Multiple studies have indicated that laughter has immunity-boosting effects and can strengthen the body's ability to fight off diseases. It can also increase the level of infection-fighting T-cells, which helps the body fight off viruses and bacteria. Laughter also increases the blood's oxygen level, allowing the body to heal and fight off illnesses.

In addition, laughter therapy can potentially reduce stress hormone levels such as cortisol and adrenaline. High levels of stress hormones can weaken the immune system, so reducing them can help the body fight off illnesses more effectively. Laughter can also help reduce inflammation, benefiting people suffering from chronic pain and diseases.

Finally, laughter therapy can help improve the quality of sleep and can be beneficial for people with insomnia. Laughter can help reduce stress and relax the body and mind, making it easier to fall asleep. It can also increase the quality of sleep, which can help the body heal and fight off illnesses.

Aids in Weight Loss

Laughter therapy has become increasingly popular in recent years to help people lose weight. Many studies have been conducted on the positive effects of laughter on weight loss, and the results have been very encouraging.

Another benefit of laughter therapy is its ability to reduce stress. Stress often triggers emotional eating and unhealthy food choices. By incorporating laughter therapy to alleviate stress, individuals may be more inclined to make healthier decisions regarding their meals. Over time, this can contribute to significant weight loss.

Laughter also helps to boost metabolism. By increasing the speed at which the body processes food, more calories are burned. This can lead to a decrease in body fat and help people to reach their weight loss goals.

In addition, laughter therapy can help to improve digestion. When people are laughing, their digestive system works much more efficiently. Enhanced digestion can support better nutrient absorption from food, potentially contributing to weight loss.

Mental Health Benefits of Laughter

One notable benefit is its ability to enhance feelings of happiness and optimism.

Laughter therapy can also help to improve cognitive functions and mental clarity. Research indicates that laughter can enhance memory and concentration, thus improving cognitive performance. It can also help reduce fatigue and confusion, helping foster mental alertness and sharpness. Additionally, laughter has been found to boost creativity and problem-solving abilities, potentially facilitating innovative thinking and effective decision-making.

It is worth noting that while laughter therapy can contribute to improved mental health and cognitive functioning, it is not a substitute for professional mental health and treatment. It should be used to aid other appropriate intervention strategies as per your needs.

Helps With Our Struggles

Laughter's contagious nature offers a valuable means of distraction and support when facing personal challenges. Hearing other people laugh can help to lift your spirits and give you a sense of optimism and hope. When we laugh with others, it can help to build relationships and create a feeling of unity. This can be very beneficial when dealing with complex problems, as we can find comfort in knowing that we are not alone in our struggles. Knowing that we have the support of those around us can make problem-solving more manageable and less daunting.

Enhances Your Mood

According to research, laughter can boost serotonin and dopamine levels, two hormones related to positive emotions. It can also help improve mood and reduce loneliness or isolation. Furthermore, it stimulates the body's production of endorphins, contributing to overall well-being.

Reduces Stress Hormones

Studies have shown that laughter therapy is effective in reducing stress hormones in the body. When we engage in laughter, our body releases endorphins, natural chemicals that promote a sense of well-being. Endorphins also reduce the production of cortisol, a hormone associated with stress.

Strengthens Relationships

Laughter therapy can also be used as a means to facilitate social interaction. Studies have shown that laughter shared among friends can help to create a stronger bond and provide a sense of shared joy. Moreover, spending positive time together builds trust and strengthens relationships. Laughter has the power to deepen bonds and make you feel more connected to friends, family, and coworkers. Additionally, humor can serve as a powerful tool for resolving past conflicts and longstanding grudges.

How to Laugh More and Have a Happy Life

In the midst of the seriousness of school and work, it is easy to overlook the importance of incorporating laughter into our lives. The following strategies will help you find ways to invite more laughter and happiness into your daily routine.

Follow a Hilarious Meme Account

Add some humor to your social media experience by following a hilarious meme account. Every time you log in, you'll be greeted with a smile.

Make a Board on Pinterest

Create a board with phrases and funny images that make you chuckle. The next time you come across an amusing web page, pin it to your board so you may refer to it the next time you're stressed.

Spend Time With Pets

Pets have a remarkable ability to bring joy and laughter into our lives. If you don't have a pet of your own, consider pet-sitting for a friend occasionally or volunteering at an animal shelter during your leisure time.

Listen to a Humorous Podcast

Listening to a humorous podcast on the way to work or school will help you start your day with a smile.

Learn to Laugh at Yourself

One of the most effective ways to increase your laughter quotient is to develop the ability to laugh at yourself. When you find yourself doing something that would typically make you angry or embarrassed, try not to take it too seriously and instead find the humor in the situation.

Change Your Environment

Your environment has a significant impact on your mood. Include items in your workspace or living space that bring back happy memories that make you chuckle, such as a photo of you and your friends from a humorous night out or a photograph of your dog dressed up in a silly costume.

Spend a Night of Laughter With Friends

Nothing beats a good laugh with friends. Do whatever makes you and your friends happy. Host a game night with friends at your home and play party games like Apples to Apples or Charades. If games aren't your thing, watch a comedy movie together or reminisce hilarious moments in your lives if you dare to share.

It's easy to forget that taking care of ourselves is one of the most important things we can do for our physical and mental well-being. When we take care of ourselves, we can better cope with everyday stresses, gain and maintain better relationships, and be more productive at work and in life.

We have explored a wealth of information in this final chapter about self-care. Remember that self-care is a skill that needs to be practiced regularly in order to be able to reap its benefits. If you can't find time in your daily schedule right now, restructure your schedule so you can make time every day to do something that makes you happy. Be it taking a bath, meditating, exercising, reading a book, or spending time with friends and family, make time to take care of yourself. We have discussed ways to incorporate self-care into your daily routine, such as positive self-affirmations, laughter therapy, relaxation techniques, and practicing mindfulness and self-compassion.

Consistently practicing healthy self-care habits can help you to embrace your true self, discover your passions and purpose, and lead a content and fulfilling life. This is what makes life truly meaningful and worthwhile!

Conclusion

At the beginning of our introduction, we peered into the life of Laura, who struggled to find a balance between her work and personal life. Both aspects were important to her, or so she thought. However, during a reflective moment at her office chair, she contemplated several profound questions. If she were to lose her job unexpectedly, could it be replaced? Possibly. If she were to lose her daughter unexpectedly, could she be replaced? Most definitely not. If something unfortunate happened to her, would her employer be able to manage without her? Most likely. If something unfortunate were to happen to her, would her daughter be able to manage without her? Hardly so.

Laura's priorities suddenly became crystal clear to her. That night, she made a personal resolution to prioritize her daughter, Avery, over her work. She also realized that taking better care of herself was a high priority. Although determined to set firm boundaries at work, Laura felt anxious and apprehensive about her manager's response, as she was not accustomed to creating conflicts or disruptions.

However, even in this moment of weakness, her daughter gave her strength. A framed photo of Avery taking her first steps at twelve months stole her attention. There would be many more milestones in Avery's life, and she didn't want to miss any more of those. With each passing moment, her fears gradually diminished, fueling her unwavering determination to chart a new course in her life.

In the following months, Laura faced difficulties in her work life. She eventually lost several accounts because she could not meet the demands and deadlines within her 40-hour work week. Her employer began to lose faith in her and would give her menial accounts with smaller bonuses while her colleagues were offered the bigger accounts. She knew she was subtly being pushed out the door.

Realizing that her current situation was no longer serving her well, Laura made the decision to explore other opportunities. She applied to several agencies within her area, but nothing seemed promising. Undeterred, she embarked on a new path and decided to start her own marketing firm with the ultimate goal of being able to work from the comfort of her home. It was rough at first, but eventually, she was able to let go of her office job with minimal loss to her income. She's still working on managing her time well, but at least she is no longer working impractical hours to the point of burnout as she had been in her previous job. In her calendar, actually important events like dance recitals and social gatherings have now replaced the never-ending monotonous meetings that she used to endure, believing it was all for her family.

Admittedly, it was a hard road to recovery, but to Laura, it was well worth the struggle. Her only regret is not having taken action sooner.

While Laura's circumstances and abilities may differ from yours, her struggles and emotions resonate with many. To a certain degree, we all have some control over how our life story will be written. Your life of burnout does not need to continue indefinitely. Just like Laura, you need to find your fire. This will help you overcome your fears and take that first step towards finding fulfillment and contentment in your life.

Now equipped with a wealth of information, you have the tools to navigate your transition. Chapter by chapter, we delved into various aspects of burnout and provided guidance to support your journey toward well-being.

In Chapter 1, we examined the physical, emotional, and behavioral signs of burnout, confirming your symptoms. Chapter 2 shed light on the red flags of a toxic workplace, including toxic positivity. Chapter 3 guided you in identifying the root causes of your burnout, exploring work and lifestyle triggers, as well as personal traits that may contribute.

Chapter 4 empowered you to shift your mindset towards fulfillment and positivity. You learned valuable strategies for balancing your work and personal life. In Chapter 5, we drew a clear line in the sand, motivating you to set healthy work boundaries, whether within a company or while working from home. We armed you with tips on effective communication with your manager, handling pushbacks, and remaining resolute in honoring your boundaries.

The final chapter placed the focus on you, the most important person in your life. By implementing self-care, self-compassion, and mindfulness practices into your daily life, you can combat the effects of burnout and restore your energy. With renewed strength, you will be better equipped to manage workplace pressures, establish non-negotiable boundaries, and embark on a new path that aligns with your personal values, leading to true fulfillment and success.

Remember, every story has the potential for a happy ending, and yours can have one too. Embrace a renewed life free from burnout and begin this new chapter today. You have the power and resilience to make it happen. You got this!

P.S. If you have found Relief From Burnout inspirational or supportive in your recovery from burnout, we would love for you to share your thoughts and feedback with us by way of an Amazon review.

P.S.S. Download the affirmation note cards for free on the www.thepagep ress.com website under Members/Toolbox.

thank you

Receive a free advanced reader copy of
our next book just by signing up at
https://mhmckinley.thepagepress.com/
burnout-rm/

References

[1] 4 *Tactics that Backfire When Dealing with a Difficult Colleague*. (2022, September 21). Harvard Business Review. https://hbr.org/2022/09/4-tactics-that-backfire-when-dealing-with-a-difficult-colleague

[2] 4 *vagus nerve exercises to transform how you handle stress*. (n.d.). Apollo Neuro. https://apolloneuro.com/blogs/news/4-vagus-nerve-exercises-to-transform-how-you-handle-stress

[3] 6 *Causes of Burnout, and How to Avoid Them*. (2021, August 27). Harvard Business Review. https://hbr.org/2019/07/6-causes-of-burnout-and-how-to-avoid-them

[4] 8 *Ways to Take Action on Mental Health Action Day – Mental Health Is Health*. (n.d.). https://www.mentalhealthishealth.us/x-ways-to-take-action-for-your-mental-health/

[5] 10 *Telltale Signs You May Be a Perfectionist*. (2023, February 14). Verywell Mind. https://www.verywellmind.com/signs-you-may-be-a-perfectionist-3145233

[5] 50 *Self-Affirmations to Help You Stay Motivated Every Day*. (2020, April 30). US Oral Surgery Management. https://www.usosm.com/employee/50-self-affirmations-to-help-you-stay-motivated-every-day/

[6] Allen, R. (2019, April 30). *Fulfillment versus Success—Which is More Important?* Roger K Allen, Conflict Management, Listening Skills, Self Empowerment. https://www.rogerkallen.com/fulfillment-versus-success/

[7] *Attention Required! | Cloudflare*. (n.d.). https://hellosalo.com/insights-ideas/overcoming-overworking-15-tips-for-taking-back-your-life/

[8] *Author Talks: Why burnout is an epidemic—and what to do about it.* (n.d.). McKinsey & Company. https://www.mckinsey.com/featured-insights/mckinsey-on-books/author-talks-why-burnout-is-an-epidemic-and-what-to-do-about-it

[9] Bakker, W. (2021, October 5). *The thin line between FOMO and a burnout*. Vox Magazine. https://www.voxweb.nl/english/the-thin-line-between-fomo-and-a-burnout

[10] Barrett, J. (2015, January 29). *Larry David, Steve Coogan and other comedians share stories of depression in new documentary*. The Independent. https://www.independent.co.uk/news/people/news/larry-david-steve-coogan-and-other-comedians-share-stories-of-depression-in-new-documentary-10009461.html

[11] Barriers to Self-Compassion. (n.d.). *Building Self-Compassion*. https://www.cci.health.wa.gov.au/~/media/CCI/Consumer-Modules/Building-Self-Compassion/Building-Self-Compassion---02---Barriers-to-Self-Compassion.pdf

[12] Blum, D. (2022, September 1). *Burnout vs Depression: How to Tell the Difference and Find Relief*. The New York Times. https://www.nytimes.com/2022/08/23/well/mind/burnout-depression-symptoms-treatment.html

[13] Brian Tracy. (2017, December 21). *How to Recover from Being Burned Out [Restore Motivation!] | Brian Tracy* [Video]. YouTube. https://www.youtube.com/watch?v=5IaT5KlzTOg

[14] Brown, L. M. (2022, June 10). *Human Giver Syndrome: The Real Reason We Are So Tired*. Lynne McLean Brown Life Coaching. https://www.lynnemcleanbrown.com/human-giver-syndrome/

[15] *Burn-out an "occupational phenomenon": International Classification of Diseases.* (2019, May 28). https://www.who.int/news/item/28-05-2019-burn-out-an-occupational-phenomenon-international-classification-of-diseases

[16] *Burnout Prevention and Treatment.* (n.d.-a). HelpGuide.org. https://www.helpguide.org/articles/stress/burnout-prevention-and-recovery.htm

[17] Colella-Graham, C. (2022, August 10). *The Rise Of Toxic Positivity, And What You Can Do About It.* Forbes. https://www.forbes.com/sites/forbeshumanresourcescouncil/2022/08/10/the-rise-of-toxic-positivity-and-what-you-can-do-about-it/?sh=4d8b16b35bf8

[18] Cook, G. (2018, March 22). *12 Tips for Time Management for Successful CEOs.* Plecto. https://www.plecto.com/blog/sales-performance/12-time-management-tips-successful-ceos-foto/

[19] Counseling, P. F. (2017, September 20). *People Pleasing, Burnout and Boundaries.* Pax Family Counseling. https://paxfamilycounseling.com/2017/09/19/people-pleasing-burnout-boundaries/

[20] D. (2022a, October 17). *8 Law of Attraction Tips from Abraham Hicks to Manifest with Ease.* The Chic Life. https://thechiclife.com/2020/02/8-law-of-attraction-tips-from-abraham-hicks-to-manifest-with-ease.html

[21] DocVita, T. (2023, February 21). *How to Talk to My Manager About Work Burnout.* DocVita. https://docvita.com/blog/how-to-tell-my-boss-that-i-am-burnt-out/

[22] Doniger, A. (2021, September 23). *The future of work is here, employee burnout needs to go.* CNBC. https://www.cnbc.com/2021/09/23/the-future-of-work-is-here-employee-burnout-needs-to-go.html

[23] Earl, M. (2020, June 1). *Success vs. Fulfillment*. Mitchell Earl. https://mitchellearl.com/success-vs-fulfillment/

[24] Editorial Team. (2022, November 11). *Stress vs. Burnout–What's the difference*. Doctor on Demand. https://doctorondemand.com/blog/mental-health/stress-vs-burnout/

[25] *FOMO and Burnout*. (n.d.). Dr. Nancy Williams. https://drnancywilliams.com/blogs/the-joyful-culture-warrior-blog/posts/6609229/fomo-and-burnout

[26] Fraga, J. (2019a, June 6). *Why the WHO's Decision to Redefine Burnout Is Important*. Healthline. https://www.healthline.com/health/mental-health/burnout-definition-world-health-organization

[27] Get Ahead by LinkedIn News. (2022, August 8). *What is Toxic Positivity in the Workplace?* https://www.linkedin.com/pulse/what-toxic-positivity-workplace-get-ahead-by-linkedin-news

[28] Gitomer, J. (2007, July 1). *Success vs. fulfillment. Which is it for you?* Jeffrey Gitomer. https://www.gitomer.com/success-vs-fulfillment-which-is-it-for-you/

[29] Goodman, R. (2021, January 22). *The Power of Self Affirmation by Dr Rick Goodman*. Dr. Rick Goodman. https://www.rickgoodman.com/power-self-affirmation/

[30] Grabarek, P. (2020, December 7). *Is Burnout Contagious?* Workr Beeing | the Science of Thriving Workplaces. https://workrbeeing.com/2020/12/06/contagious-burnout/

[31] Harker, N. (2020, March 20). *How People-pleasing Brought Me to the Brink of Burnout*. Thrive Global. https://community.thriveglobal.com/how-people-pleasing-brought-me-to-the-brink-of-burnout/

[32] Havrilesky, H. (2022, August 24). *Overcoming Burnout Is About More Than Endless Self-Care*. Bustle. https://www.bustle.com/wellness/overcoming-burnout-self-care

[33] Houston, R. (2021, February 25). *Success & Fulfillment*. Speaking With a Purpose. https://www.speakingwithapurpose.com/success-fulfillment/

[34] *How Your Personality Traits Can Put You at Risk for Burnout*. (2020, October 22). Verywell Mind. https://www.verywellmind.com/mental-burnout-personality-traits-3144514

[35] HRZone. (2013, July 29). *What is Work-life Balance?* https://www.hrzone.com/hr-glossary/what-is-work-life-balance

[36] Hwang, J. (2022, February 18). *How to Set Work-Life Boundaries When You Work From Home*. Skillcrush. https://skillcrush.com/blog/work-from-home-boundaries/

[37] *inc.com.* (n.d.-a). https://www.inc.com/marcel-schwantes/neuroscience-says-doing-these-activities-will-help-keep-your-brain-more-focused.html

[38] *inc.com.* (n.d.-b). https://www.inc.com/benjamin-p-hardy/how-to-change-how-you-talk-and-see-to-yourself.html

[39] James, T. (2022, July 4). *30 Self-Care Tips: How to Avoid Sickness, Burnout, and Exhaustion*. Tiny Buddha. https://tinybuddha.com/blog/30-self-care-tips-how-to-avoid-sickness-burnout-and-exhaustion/

[40] Jenkins, R. (2022, March 3). *What a Workplace Loneliness Expert Wants You to Know About the Emotion*. Entrepreneur. https://www.entrepreneur.com/leadership/what-a-workplace-loneliness-expert-wants-you-to-know-about/418947

[41] Jhamnani, P. (2020, June 23). *Abraham Hick's Pivoting Technique*. https://www.linkedin.com/pulse/abraham-hicks-pivoting-technique-pooja-jhamnani

[42] Jun, P. (2012, November 5). *The Real Meaning of Success*. Lifehack. https://www.lifehack.org/articles/work/the-true-meaning-of-success.html

[43] *Just a moment. . . (n.d.)*. https://www.indeed.com/career-advic e/career-development/not-being-recognized-at-work

[44] K. (2015, February 22). *Is it self-indulgent to be self-compassionate? by Kristin Neff*. Self-Compassion. https://self-compassion.org/is-it -self-indulgent-to-be-self-compassionate/

[45] Kataria, V. (2021, December 13). *The Toxic Effect of Glorifying Hard Work - The Startup*. Medium. https://medium.com/swlh/the-toxic -effect-of-glorifying-hard-work-7eba82087432

[46] Kelly, J. (2021, April 5). *Indeed Study Shows That Worker Burnout Is At Frighteningly High Levels: Here Is What You Need To Do Now*. F   o   r   b   e   s   . https://www.forbes.com/sites/jackkelly/2021/04/05/indeed-stud y-shows-that-worker-burnout-is-at-frighteningly-high-levels-here -is-what-you-need-to-do-now/?sh=2a73672d23bb

[47] Khaire, N. (2021, December 12). *The Truth Why Positive Affirmations Are So Powerful*. Medium. https://writerempire.medium.com/t he-truth-why-positive-affirmations-are-so-powerful-74fc46d152ec

[48] Knight, C. (2021, September 29). *Burn Out And The Importance Of Self-Compassion And Self-Care*. https://psychprofessionals.com.au/ burn-out-and-the-importance-of-self-compassion-and-self-care/

[49] Korn, J. (2021, November 1). *Toxic Positivity In The Workplace*. Forbes. https://www.forbes.com/sites/juliawuench/2021/11 /01/toxic-positivity-in-the-workplace/?sh=3619fe91e6f8

[50] Kristenson, S. (2022, July 14). *14 Toxic Positivity Examples (And How to Stop Doing Them)*. Happier Human. https://www.happierhu man.com/toxic-positivity-examples/

[51] *Learning to Relax*. (2018, July 22). Rogel Cancer Center | University of Michigan. https://www.rogelcancercenter.org/breaking-habi ts-beating-us/learning-relax

[52] *Let the Law of Attraction Help You With Positive Change.* (2022, November 7). Verywell Mind. https://www.verywellmind.com/understanding-and-using-the-law-of-attraction-3144808

[53] Levitt, M. (2020, March 20). *How Time Management Can Prevent Burnout.* Thrive Global. https://community.thriveglobal.com/how-time-management-can-prevent-burnout/

[54] LiquidPlanner, I. (2022a, August 11). *Time Management Techniques to Prevent Burnout.* LiquidPlanner. https://www.liquidplanner.com/blog/time-management-techniques-to-prevent-burnout/

[55] Livingston, M. (2022, October 30). *Naturally Reduce Stress With These 8 Anxiety-Fighting Exercises.* CNET. https://www.cnet.com/health/fitness/naturally-reduce-stress-with-these-8-anxiety-fighting-exercises/

[56] Louise, E. (2022, April 25). *17 Second Manifestation: Is this the secret to LOA success?* Through the Phases. https://www.throughthephases.com/17-second-manifestation/

[57] Lutz, J. (2018, February 28). *When You Talk To Yourself It Matters: How To Master Your Self Talk.* Forbes. https://www.forbes.com/sites/jessicalutz/2018/02/28/how-you-talk-to-yourself-matters-how-to-master-your-self-talk/?sh=48d32f2e4772

[58] Maynard, S. C. P. C. (2022a, January 28). *How Self Care Can Help Prevent Burnout.* Spring Health. https://springhealth.com/blog/how-self-care-prevents-burnout/

[59] MBA Skool Team. (2021a, August 15). *Work Life Balance - Meaning, Importance, Steps & Example.* MBA Skool. https://www.mbaskool.com/business-concepts/human-resources-hr-terms/7045-work-life-balance.html

[60] Medmastery. (2021, March 22). *How to identify signs of burnout* [Video]. YouTube. https://www.youtube.com/watch?v=JZ5CW5qsktM

[61] Mental Health UK. (2022, July 1). *Burnout.* https://mentalhealth-uk.org/burnout/

[62] Montañez, R. (2019, August 19). *3 Essential Tactics For Conquering Sleep Deprivation And Burnout.* Forbes. https://www.forbes.com/sites/rachelmontanez/2019/08/18/3-essential-tactics-for-conquering-sleep-deprivation-and-burnout/?sh=2f5a245fce97

[63] Morrison, C. (2022, March 11). *16 Employee Burnout Statistics You Can't Ignore.* EveryoneSocial. https://everyonesocial.com/blog/employee-burnout-statistics/

[64] *NCBI - WWW Error Blocked Diagnostic.* (n.d.). https://www.ncbi.nlm.nih.gov/pmc/articles/PMC8648575/

[65] Nigeria, G. (2016, March 17). *Understanding the true meaning of success.* The Guardian Nigeria News - Nigeria and World News. https://guardian.ng/features/understanding-the-true-meaning-of-success/

[66] *Passion and burnout.* (n.d.). Codecentric. https://blog.codecentric.de/passion-and-burnout

[67] Pelta, R. (2022, February 21). *How to Set Boundaries Between Work and Home.* FlexJobs Job Search Tips and Blog. https://www.flexjobs.com/blog/post/maintain-boundaries-between-work-and-home-telecommute/

[68] Perry, 1. (2022, November 13). *Burnout and Boundaries: Knowing when enough is enough.* Fuller Life Family Therapy. https://fullerlifefamilytherapy.org/burnout-boundaries/

[69] Price, D. (2019a, November 9). *Burnout Contagion.* CQ Net - Management Skills for Everyone! https://www.ckju.net/en/dossier/burnout-contagion-managing-and-reducing-socially-transmitted-burnout

[70] *psycom.net*. (n.d.). https://www.psycom.net/how-to-be-happy

[71] R. (2022b, April 27). *Success vs. Fulfillment*. International Coach Academy. https://coachcampus.com/coach-portfolios/power-tools/success-vs-fulfillment/

[72] Rampton, J. (2020b, January 28). *How Time Management Can Help You Avoid Burnout*. Entrepreneur. https://www.entrepreneur.com/living/how-time-management-can-help-you-avoid-burnout/345091

[73] Roberts, C. (2020, February 16). *How to set healthy boundaries at work to avoid burnout*. CNET. https://www.cnet.com/health/how-to-set-healthy-boundaries-at-work-to-avoid-burnout/

[74] Rose, H. (2021, October 26). *How to harness the power of self-affirmation*. Ness Labs. https://nesslabs.com/self-affirmation

[75] Sanfilippo, M. (2023, February 21). *How to Improve Your Work-Life Balance Today*. Business News Daily. https://www.businessnewsdaily.com/5244-improve-work-life-balance-today.html

[76] Sheehan, H. (2022, January 5). *How CEOs Manage Their Time*. Fellow.app. https://fellow.app/blog/productivity/how-ceos-manage-their-time/

[77] Smith, J. (2013, September 18). 15 *Signs That Your Job May Be At Risk--And What To Do If It Is*. Forbes. https://www.forbes.com/sites/jacquelynsmith/2013/09/18/15-signs-that-your-job-may-be-at-risk-and-what-to-do-if-it-is/?sh=288e5ca95e5b

[78] Spicer, A. (2019, January 29). *Why we must resist the cult of 'performative workaholism.'* The Guardian. https://www.theguardian.com/money/shortcuts/2019/jan/28/work-life-balance-thankgoditsmonday

[79] Staff, C. G. R. C. (2021, January 15). 30 *Self Care Ideas for Burnout*. CGRC. https://cgrc.org/blog/untitled-4/

[80] *Stress relief from laughter? It's no joke.* (2021, July 29). Mayo Clinic. https://www.mayoclinic.org/healthy-lifestyle/stress-management/in-depth/stress-relief/art-20044456

[81] TEDx Talks. (2022, March 28). *How to Turn Burnout into Breakthrough | Oma Agbai | TEDxColeParkStudio* [Video]. YouTube. https://www.youtube.com/watch?v=zw1tZ0dhs9I

[82] *Ten Things You Can Do for Your Mental Health | University Health Service.* (n.d.). https://uhs.umich.edu/tenthings

[83] Tesema, M. (n.d.-b). *The Type of Burnout We Rarely Talk About.* Shine. https://advice.theshineapp.com/articles/burnout/

[84] *The Five Myths of Self-Compassion.* (n.d.). Greater Good. https://greatergood.berkeley.edu/article/item/the_five_myths_of_self_compassion

[85] *The True Meaning of Success.* (2021, November 6). Steve Rose, PhD. https://steverosephd.com/the-true-meaning-of-success/

[86] Therapy, M. (2019, March 15). *The Difference Between Working Hard and Burning Out: Modern Therapy.* https://moderntherapy.online/blog-2/2019/3/2/the-difference-between-working-hard-and-burning-out

[87] Thevapalan, A. (2021, December 15). *How Many Times Do You Unlock Your Phone Every Day? - Live Your Life On Purpose.* Medium. https://medium.com/live-your-life-on-purpose/how-many-times-do-you-unlock-your-phone-every-day-c6971627223c

[88] Thompson, R. (2021a, October 7). *How To Set Boundaries At Work.* Mashable India. https://in.mashable.com/life/25180/how-to-set-boundaries-at-work

[89] TODAY. (2019, May 28). *Burnout Is Now A Legitimate Diagnosis: Here Are The Symptoms And How To Treat It | TODAY* [Video]. YouTube. https://www.youtube.com/watch?v=GI0BX35BJ-0

[90] Treasure, A. (2022, March 14). *Self-Care is Not the Solution for Burnout*. The Beautiful Truth. https://thebeautifultruth.org/mental-health/self-care-is-not-the-solution-for-burnout/

[91] Ullah, R. (2020, December 3). *What Are Positive Affirmations (And Why Are They Powerful)?* Lifehack. https://www.lifehack.org/515761/the-power-positive-affirmations

[92] W. (2022c, September 7). *Toxic Positivity Cultures*. Wellable. https://www.wellable.co/blog/perpetual-positivity-in-the-workplace-may-be-toxic/

[93] Wedgwood, J. (2022, September 21). *The Importance of Work-Life Balance*. The Happiness Index. https://thehappinessindex.com/blog/importance-work-life-balance/

[94] *What is Self-Compassion?* (2016, January 1). GoStrengths! https://gostrengths.com/what-is-self-compassion/

[95] *When Passion Leads to Burnout*. (2021, August 27). Harvard Business Review. https://hbr.org/2019/07/when-passion-leads-to-burnout

[96] *Why Brain Overload Happens | Lesley University*. (n.d.). https://lesley.edu/article/why-brain-overload-happens

[97] *Why is employee burnout on the rise globally? | Australian Institute of Health & Safety*. (n.d.). https://www.aihs.org.au/news-and-publications/news/why-employee-burnout-rise-globally

[98] Wong, K. (2023a, January 19). *How To Manifest In 17 Seconds By Abraham Hicks*. The Millennial Grind. https://millennial-grind.com/how-to-manifest-in-17-seconds-in-5-steps/

[99] Wong, K. (2023b, January 19). *The 3 P's of Affirmations*. The Millennial Grind. https://millennial-grind.com/the-3-ps-of-affirmations/

[100] Z. (2022d, April 19). *What Is Burnout?* Cleveland Clinic. https://health.clevelandclinic.org/signs-of-burnout/

[101] Healthy Mind, Healthy Life: 7 famous people that have overcome burnout .... https://navigator-business-optimizer.com/2020/11/healthy-mind-healthy-life-7-famous-people-that-have-overcome-burnout/.

Made in the USA
Columbia, SC
16 July 2023